COSTS AND REVENUES

STANDARD LOAN

thyr Tydfil Learning Resources Centre
Tel: (01685) 726000

Qualifications and Credit Framework

Level 3 Diploma in Accounting

MERTHYR TYDFIL COLLEGE

25456

British Library Cataloguing-in-Publication Data

A catalogue record for this book is available from the British Library.

Published by
Kaplan Publishing UK
Unit 2, The Business Centre
Molly Millars Lane
Wokingham
Berkshire
RG41 2QZ

ISBN 978-0-85732-217-3

The text in this material and any others made available by any Kaplan Group company does not amount to advice on a particular matter and should not be taken as such. No reliance should be placed on the content as the basis for any investment or other decision or in connection with any advice given to third parties. Please consult your appropriate professional adviser as necessary. Kaplan Publishing Limited and all other Kaplan group companies expressly disclaim all liability to any person in respect of any losses or other claims, whether direct, indirect, incidental, consequential or otherwise arising in relation to the use of such materials.

© Kaplan Financial Limited, 2010

Printed in Great Britain by WM Print Ltd, Walsall.

We are grateful to the Association of Accounting Technicians for permission to reproduce past assessment materials and example tasks based on the new syllabus. The solutions to past answers and similar activities in the style of the new syllabus have been prepared by Kaplan Publishing.

All rights reserved. No part of this publication may be reproduced, stored in a retrieval system, or transmitted, in any form or by any means, electronic, mechanical, photocopying, recording or otherwise, without the prior written permission of Kaplan Publishing.

CONTENTS

STUDY TEXT AND WORKBOOK

INTRODUCTION

HOW TO USE THESE MATERIALS

These Kaplan Publishing learning materials have been carefully designed to make your learning experience as easy as possible and to give you the best chance of success in your AAT assessments.

They contain a number of features to help you in the study process.

The sections on the Unit Guide, the Assessment and Study Skills should be read before you commence your studies.

They are designed to familiarise you with the nature and content of the assessment and to give you tips on how best to approach your studies.

STUDY TEXT

This study text has been specially prepared for the revised AAT qualification introduced in July 2010.

It is written in a practical and interactive style:

- key terms and concepts are clearly defined

- all topics are illustrated with practical examples with clearly worked solutions based on sample tasks provided by the AAT in the new examining style

- frequent practice activities throughout the chapters ensure that what you have learnt is regularly reinforced

- 'pitfalls' and 'examination tips' help you avoid commonly made mistakes and help you focus on what is required to perform well in your examination.

- clear advice as to which practice activities can be completed is given at the end of each chapter

WORKBOOK

The workbook comprises:

A question bank of practice activities with solutions, to reinforce the work covered in each chapter.

The questions are divided into their relevant chapters and students may either attempt these questions as they work through the textbook, or leave some or all of these until they have completed the textbook as a final revision of what they have studied

ICONS

The study chapters include the following icons throughout.

They are designed to assist you in your studies by identifying key definitions and the points at which you can test yourself on the knowledge gained.

 Definition

These sections explain important areas of Knowledge which must be understood and reproduced in an assessment

 Example

The illustrative examples can be used to help develop an understanding of topics before attempting the activity exercises

 Activity

These are exercises which give the opportunity to assess your understanding of all the assessment areas.

 Test your knowledge

At the end of each chapter these boxes will direct you to the Practice Activities that you can attempt after studying the chapter.

KAPLAN PUBLISHING

UNIT GUIDE

Cost and Revenues is divided into two units but for the purposes of assessment these units will be combined.

Principles of Costing (Knowledge)

4 credits

Providing Cost and Revenue Information (Skills)

4 credits

Purpose of the units

The AAT has stated that the general purpose of these units is to enable learners to understand the role of costing in an organisation and how organisations use cost and revenue information for decision making.

Learning objectives

On completion of these units the learner will be able to:

- demonstrate an understanding of the role of costing within the organisation

- advise on the most appropriate costing methods to use within an organisation

- understand the principles of using costing as a decision making tool

- record and analyse information relating to costs

- apportion costs according to organisational requirements

- correctly identify any significant deviations and report these to management

Learning Outcomes and Assessment criteria

The unit consists of six learning outcomes, three for Knowledge and three for Skills, which are further broken down into Assessment criteria. These are set out in the following table with Learning Outcomes in bold type and Assessment criteria listed underneath each Learning Outcome. Reference is also made to the relevant chapter within the text.

Knowledge

To perform this unit effectively you will need to know and understand the following:

		Chapter
1	**Demonstrate an understanding of the role of costing within the organisation**	
1.1	Explain the purpose of internal reporting and providing accurate information to management in terms of decision making, planning and control	Throughout
1.2	Explain the relationship between the various costing and accounting systems within an organisation	1, 2, 3, 5, 8
1.3	Identify the responsibility centres, cost centres, profit centres and investment centres within an organisation	1
1.4	Explain the characteristics of different types of cost classifications and their use in costing	1, 9
2	**Advise on the most appropriate costing methods to use within an organisation**	
2.1	Identify the most appropriate methods of stock control and valuation	2
2.2	Identify costs and the correct classification	1, 5, 9, 10
	• fixed	
	• variable	
	• Semi-variable	
	• stepped	
2.3	Identify the differences between marginal and absorption costing	5

Skills

To perform this unit effectively you will need to be able to do the following.

KAPLAN PUBLISHING

Delivery guidance

The AAT have provided delivery guidance giving further details of the way in which the unit will be assessed.

Demonstrate an understanding of the role of costing within the organisation.

Students need to know and understand the different ways in which organisations record, analyse and report costs and revenues. Such costs and revenues are often treated differently from one organisation to the next - depending on the accepted practice within the business sector the organisation operates in, and on the specific measurement rules chosen by the individual organisation.

Students should be able to comment on compliance with organisational policies, such as those for inventory (stock) control, and labour payment rates; must understand the significance of these different ways of dealing with cost and revenue information, and indirectly demonstrate knowledge by skill by applying them in relevant circumstances.

Management needs accurate information, based on an understanding of cost behaviour. This information will be used for both short-term decision making (e.g. break-even analysis techniques) and long-term decision making (e.g. investment appraisal techniques); planning (e.g. forecasting changes in profitability as activity levels change); and control (e.g. through variance analysis).

Students need to understand the relationship between the various costing and accounting systems in an organisation. This includes the relationship between the materials costing system and the inventory control system; the relationship between the labour costing system and the payroll accounting system; and the relationship between the overheads costing system and the accounting system.

Students need to know and understand the difference between cost, profit and investment centres; and to be able to identify which of these applies to different parts of an organisation. They also need to know and understand the principles behind and, where appropriate, the makeup of cost objects; direct costs; indirect costs and the elements of cost (e.g prime cost and production cost).

The behavioural characteristics of costs are summarised below.

Advise on the most appropriate costing methods to use within an organisation.

Students should be able to identify and explain the principles behind First In First out (FIFO), Last In First Out (LIFO) and Weighted Average Cost (AVCO) methods of inventory control and valuation.

They need to know and understand the different methods that organisations use to control inventories, such as inventory buffers (buffer stocks), lead times, minimum/maximum order quantities and the Economic Order Quantity (EOQ).

They need to be able to identify how particular costs would be classified, based upon their short term cost behaviour, and the implications of cost behaviour for cost recording, reporting and analysis. Cost classifications include fixed, variable, step-fixed and semi-variable.

They should also appreciate that such a classification of costs holds only in the short term, and that in the long term all costs are variable.

Students need to know and understand the principles of marginal (variable) and absorption (full absorption) costing. They should understand the causal effects on reported profits, and closing inventories in any one period due to the choice of costing principle; and that over the life of an organisation there is no effect on overall reported profits.

They should also understand the circumstances in which marginal costing is more appropriate (e.g. short term decision making), and those in which absorption costing is more appropriate (e.g. statutory financial reporting).

They should also understand the difference between product costs and period costs.

Students should be able indirectly demonstrate knowledge through the application of skills, by making calculations of product costs and reported profits on both principles.

Students need to be able to identify, explain and make calculations for both the direct and step down bases of allocation and apportionment of overheads. They should appreciate the difference between allocations and apportionments.

They must know and understand the different bases of absorption. These are confined to machine hours and direct labour hours for manufacturers; and to appropriate bases (e.g. miles travelled for a bus company) for service sector organisations. They should be able to choose the most appropriate basis for a particular organisation, and to justify their choice of basis.

An understanding is required of appropriate organisational costing systems - job, batch, unit, process and service costing. Students should be aware that the choice of system would depend on the business sector of the organisation. (E.g. a shipbuilder is likely to use job costing whereas an oil refinery is likely to use process costing). Process and job costing systems represent the extreme ends of a continuum, and many organisations need a combination of these two elements (as in batch costing).

Students should know and understand the reasons behind, and the implications of, classifying the costs of inventory at different stages. This includes understanding the recording of different stages of processed inventory in the accounting records, and that equivalent unit calculations (see below) are made in this context.

Understand the principles of using costing as a decision making tool.

Students must be able to identify, explain and understand the effects of changes in activity levels on unit product and service costs, revenues and profits. This requires an understanding of cost behaviour as set out above.

Knowledge and understanding is required of the concepts of discounting, net present cost, net present value and internal rate of return. Students should be able to explain the differences between, and advantages/disadvantages of, net present value and internal rate of return. Knowledge of discounted payback is not required.

Students should be able to identify and explain relevant (avoidable) and irrelevant (unavoidable) costs in the context of short-term decision making.

They should be able to identify and explain the principles underpinning break-even (CVP) analysis. This includes identification, explanations and calculations of break-even units; break-even revenue; margin of safety units; margin of safety revenue; target profit units; and target profit revenues.

Students should be able to identify and explain the principles underpinning limited factor analysis, for a single limiting factor. (Knowledge of linear programming is not required).

Students should be able to interpret calculations of payback, net present cost, and net present value. They should be able to explain the meaning of these terms and of the results of calculations. Tasks requiring Internal Rate of Return calculations will not be set, but students should be aware of its meaning (see above).

Record and analyse information relating to costs.

Students must be able to record inventories (stocks) in inventory records, and deal with labour cost calculations in payroll calculation sheets and in other methods of presentation.

They need to be able to prepare and explain journal entries for material, labour and overheads.

Students must be able to interpret and explain the processes set out above.

They should be able to undertake calculations for FIFO and AVCO methods of inventory control and valuation, including analysis of the closing balance. They should be able to advise management what the effects on reported profits and inventory values are of using each method in different circumstances, such as when inventory costs are increasing or decreasing.

They should be able to analyse the different methods that organisations use to control inventories, such as inventory buffers, lead times, minimum/maximum order quantities and the Economic Order Quantity (EOQ). Calculations may be required for all of these methods, including EOQ.

Students should be able to undertake calculations based on cost behaviour (fixed, variable, step-fixed and semi-variable), including using the high/low method.

Process costing will be examined to the following extent:

- Students should be able to explain and prepare calculations for the following process costing terms: normal loss; abnormal loss; abnormal gain.

- There will be no more than two processes.

- Process accounts will be required, covering the terms in the previous paragraph, where there is no closing work in progress. This will include scrap sales.

- Unit cost calculations for equivalent units where there is closing or opening work in progress, but not both and not including process losses.

- Neither by-products nor joint products will be examined.

Apportion costs according to organisational requirements.

Students should be able to allocate costs to responsibility centres where these have entirely incurred the relevant cost. They should be able to make primary apportionments to responsibility centres where these have shared the benefits of the relevant cost.

They should then be able to make secondary apportionments from cost centres to profit/investment centres using either the direct or step down methods.

Students should be able to undertake calculations on an appropriate basis leading to final budgeted overhead absorption rates; and must be able to identify, interpret and make calculations of under and over recovery (absorption) of overheads.

They should understand the significance of these and how they are recorded in the organisation's Income Statement (Profit & Loss account). Students should recognise the arbitrary nature of these methods under traditional costing systems; and the need to review and perhaps change them as the organisation changes over time. (E.g. As a company adds more automation it may be appropriate to change from a labour hour to a machine hour basis of absorption).

Students must be able to prepare, and explain, journals for posting under and over absorptions.

Students should be able to consult with staff in operational departments as well as with specialist accounting and management personnel. This may be examined by a brief 'report' as set out below.

Correctly identify any significant deviations and report these to management.

Students should be able to identify cost and revenue variances for:

- Direct materials.

- Direct labour.

- Fixed overheads.

- Sales

The sub-division of these variances (into e.g price and usage) will not be examined.

They should be able to reconcile the budgeted and actual costs and revenues, using the variances set out above.

'Budget costs and revenues' refers to both fixed and flexed budgets; and students are expected to be competent in using either approach in this context. Flexed budgets will not involve semi-variable cost calculations.

Students should be able to explain the meaning and significance of the above variances. This includes being able to explain the likely causes and effects of each; and should be able to advise management of ways of addressing significant deviations from budget. (E.g. an adverse material variance may be resolved by e.g. reducing the amount of materials wasted or buying it at a cheaper price)

Students need to be able to identify, explain and make calculations based upon different types of short term cost behaviour. They should be able to produce short term forecasts based on short term cost behaviour classifications; and long term forecasts based on all costs being purely variable.

They should be able to categorise costs as direct or indirect; and as relevant and irrelevant.

They should be able to make calculations based on break-even (CVP) analysis. This includes identification, explanations and calculations of break-even units; break-even revenue; margin of safety units; margin of safety revenue; target profit units; and target profit revenues.

Students should be able to make calculations based on a single limiting factor. (Knowledge of linear programming is not required).

Students should be able to undertake calculations of payback, net present cost, and net present value. They should also be able to explain the meaning of these terms and of the results of their calculations.

Tasks requiring Internal rate of return calculations will not be set, but students should be aware of its meaning (see above).

Prepare reports in an appropriate format and present these to management within the required timescales. Students may be asked in any task to produce a written memo, e-mail or report to advise of their findings.

THE ASSESSMENT

The format of the assessment

The assessment will be divided into two sections.

Section 1 covers:

- Calculations and/or explanations relating to inventory control

- Cost accounting journals

- Direct labour cost

- Allocation and apportionment of indirect costs to responsibility centres

- Overhead absorption rates including under and over absorption

There are five independent tasks in this section

Section 2 covers:

- Calculations and /or explanations relating to changes in unit costs/profits as activity levels change and profit/loss by product

- Break-even (CVP) analysis

- Limiting factor decision making

- Process costing

- Reconciling budget and actual costs and revenues by means of flexible or fixed budgets

- Capital investment appraisal

There are five independent tasks in this section

Learners will normally be assessed by computer based assessment (CBA), which will include extended writing tasks, and will be required to demonstrate competence in both sections of the assessment.

Time allowed

The time allowed for this assessment is **150 minutes.**

STUDY SKILLS

Preparing to study

Devise a study plan

Determine which times of the week you will study.

Split these times into sessions of at least one hour for study of new material. Any shorter periods could be used for revision or practice.

Put the times you plan to study onto a study plan for the weeks from now until the assessment and set yourself targets for each period of study – in your sessions make sure you cover the whole course, activities and the associated questions in the workbook at the back of the manual.

If you are studying more than one unit at a time, try to vary your subjects as this can help to keep you interested and see subjects as part of wider knowledge.

When working through your course, compare your progress with your plan and, if necessary, re-plan your work (perhaps including extra sessions) or, if you are ahead, do some extra revision / practice questions.

Effective studying

Active reading

You are not expected to learn the text by rote, rather, you must understand what you are reading and be able to use it to pass the assessment and develop good practice.

A good technique is to use SQ3Rs – Survey, Question, Read, Recall, Review:

1   **Survey the chapter**

     Look at the headings and read the introduction, knowledge, skills and content, so as to get an overview of what the chapter deals with.

2   **Question**

     Whilst undertaking the survey ask yourself the questions you hope the chapter will answer for you.

3   Read

Read through the chapter thoroughly working through the activities and, at the end, making sure that you can meet the learning objectives highlighted on the first page.

4   Recall

At the end of each section and at the end of the chapter, try to recall the main ideas of the section / chapter without referring to the text. This is best done after short break of a couple of minutes after the reading stage.

5   Review

Check that your recall notes are correct.

You may also find it helpful to re-read the chapter to try and see the topic(s) it deals with as a whole.

Note taking

Taking notes is a useful way of learning, but do not simply copy out the text.

The notes must:

- be in your own words
- be concise
- cover the key points
- well organised
- be modified as you study further chapters in this text or in related ones.

Trying to summarise a chapter without referring to the text can be a useful way of determining which areas you know and which you don't.

Three ways of taking notes

1   Summarise the key points of a chapter

2   Make linear notes

A list of headings, subdivided with sub-headings listing the key points.

If you use linear notes, you can use different colours to highlight key points and keep topic areas together.

Use plenty of space to make your notes easy to use.

KAPLAN PUBLISHING

3   **Try a diagrammatic form**

The most common of which is a mind map.

To make a mind map, put the main heading in the centre of the paper and put a circle around it.]

Draw lines radiating from this to the main sub-headings which again have circles around them.

Continue the process from the sub-headings to sub-sub-headings.

Highlighting and underlining

You may find it useful to underline or highlight key points in your study text – but do be selective.

You may also wish to make notes in the margins.

Revision phase

Kaplan has produced material specifically designed for your final examination preparation for this unit.

These include pocket revision notes and a bank of revision questions specifically in the style of the new syllabus.

Further guidance on how to approach the final stage of your studies is given in these materials.

Further reading

In addition to this text, you should also read the "Student section" of the "Accounting Technician" magazine every month to keep abreast of any guidance from the examiners.

Terminology for CRS

There are different terms used to mean the same thing – you will need to be aware of both sets of terminology.

UK GAAP	IAS
Profit and Loss	Income Statement
Sales	Revenue
Balance Sheet	Statement of Financial Position
Fixed Assets	Non-current Assets
Current Assets	Property, Plant and Equipment
Stock	Inventory
Trade Debtors	Trade Receivables
Trade Creditors	Trade Payables
Capital	Equity
Profit	Retained Earnings

Principles of cost accounting

1

Introduction

This chapter considers the basic principles of management accounting and management information.

KNOWLEDGE

Explain the purpose of internal reporting and providing accurate information to management in terms of decision making, planning and control (1.1)

Explain the relationship between the various costing and accounting systems within an organisation (1.2)

Identify the responsibility centres, cost centres, profit centres and investment centres within an organisation (1.3)

Explain the characteristics of different types of cost classifications and their use in costing (1.4)

Identify costs and the correct classification

– Fixed
– Variable
– Semi-variable
– Stepped (2.2)

Explain the effect of changing activity levels on unit costs (3.1)

SKILLS

Record and analyse costs in accordance with the organisation's costing procedures (1.1)

Analyse cost information for materials, labour and expenses (1.2)

CONTENTS

1 Financial accounting, management accounting and cost accounting

1.1 Introduction

Most business entities, whether large or small, generate large numbers of different types of transaction. To make sense of those transactions, they need to be recorded, summarised and analysed. In all businesses, it is the accounts department that performs these tasks.

From the raw data of the business's transactions, accountants provide **information for a wide range of interested parties**. Each party requires, however, slightly different information, dependent upon their interest in the business.

1.2 Financial accounting

Accountants provide information to **external groups**, such as the owners of the business and HM Revenue and Customs.

Financial accounting could be described in simple terms as **keeping score**. The financial accounts produced are a **historic record** of transactions and are presented in a standard format laid down in law. These normally include

- A statement of financial position (also known as a balance sheet)
- An income statement (also known as a profit and loss account)

Such statements are normally only produced **once or twice a year**.

Financial accounting is not, however, the only type of accounting. The other main type is management accounting.

1.3 Management accounting

Management accounting provides information for **internal users**, such as the managers of the business.

Management accounting compares **actual results with predicted results** and tries to use information to make further predictions about the future.

It also provides information which managers can use to make **decisions**.

Management accounts can be produced in **any format** that is useful to the business and tend to be produced frequently, for instance **every month**.

1.4 The aims of management accounting

The aim of management accounting is to assist management in the following areas of running a business.

- **Planning**

  For example, through the preparation of annual budgets. This is a key aspect of management accounting.

- **Co-ordinating**

  Planning enables all departments to be co-ordinated and to work together.

- **Controlling**

  The comparison of actual results with the budget helps to identify areas where operations are not running according to plan.

  Investigating the causes, and acting on the results of that investigation, help to control the activities of the business.

- **Communicating**

  Preparing budgets that are distributed to department managers helps to communicate the aims of the busienss to those managers.

- **Motivating**

  Management accounts include targets. These should motivate managers (and staff) and improve their performance.

  If the target is too difficult, however, it is likely to demotivate and it is unlikely to be achieved.

1.5 Useful management information

For **management information** to be of use to a particular group of managers, it must have the following attributes:

- **Relevant to their responsibilities**. For example, a production manager will want information about stocks, production levels, production performance, etc within his particular department.

- **Relevant to particular decisions**. For example, if deciding whether to close a division, managers would need to know the likely costs including lost sales, likely redundancies and so on.

- **Timely**. Information has to be up-to-date to be of any value.

- **Value**. The benefits of having the information must outweigh the cost of producing it.

1.6 Cost accounting

Cost accounting is usually a large part of management accounting. As its name suggests, it is concerned with **establishing costs**. It developed within manufacturing businesses where costs are most difficult to isolate and analyse.

Cost accounting is primarily directed at enabling management to perform the functions of **planning, control** and **decision making:**

(a) determining costs and profits during a control period

(b) valuing stocks of raw materials, work in progress and finished goods, and controlling stock levels

(c) preparing budgets, forecasts and other control data for a forthcoming control period

(d) creating a reporting system which enables managers to take corrective action where necessary to control costs

(e) providing information for decision-making such as pricing, for example.

Items (a) and (b) are traditional **cost accounting roles**; (c) to (e) extend into management accounting.

Cost accounting is not confined to the environment of manufacturing, although it is in this area that it is most fully developed. **Service industries, central and local government, and even accountancy and legal practices** make profitable use of cost accounting information. Furthermore, it is not restricted purely to manufacturing and operating costs, but also to administration, selling and distribution and research and development.

Be prepared for non-manufacturing scenarios in the computer based assessments.

2 Terminology – cost units and cost centres

2.1 Cost units

To help with the above purposes of planning, control and decision making, businesses often need to calculate a cost per unit of output.

A key question, however, is what exactly we mean by a "unit of output", or **"cost unit"**. This will mean different things to different businesses but we always looks at what the business produces.

- A car manufacturer will want to determine the cost of each car and probably different components as well.

- In a printing firm, the cost unit could be the specific customer order.

- For a paint manufacturer, the unit could be a litre of paint.

- An accountancy firm will want to know the costs incurred for each client. To help with this it is common to calculate the cost per hour of chargeable time spent by staff.

- A hospital might wish to calculate the cost per patient treated, the cost of providing a bed for each day or the cost of an operation, say.

2.2 Cost centres

A **cost centre** is a small part of a business for which costs are determined. This varies from business to business but could include any of the following:

- The Research and Development department

- The Human Resources function

- A warehouse

- A factory in a particular location

It is important to recognise that cost centre costs are necessary for control purposes, as well as for relating costs to cost units. This is because the manager of a cost centre will be responsible for the costs incurred.

 Activity 1

Suggest **ONE** suitable cost unit and **TWO** cost centres for a school.

2.3 Cost, profit and investment centres

Some businesses use the term "cost centre" in a more precise way than that given above:

- A **cost centre** is when the manager of the centre (department or division or location or...) is responsible for costs but not revenue or investment.

  For example, a research and development department.

- A **profit centre** is when the manager of the centre (department or division or location or...) is responsible for costs and revenues but not investment.

  For example, a local supermarket where the main Board makes investment decisions.

- An **investment centre** is when the manager of the centre (usually a division) is responsible for costs and revenues and the level of investment in the division.

  For example, the US subsidiary of a global firm. The CEO would probably have authority to open new factories, close others and so on.

3 Cost classification

3.1 Types of cost classification

Costs can be **classified** (collected into logical groups) in many ways. The particular classification selected will depend upon the purpose for which the resulting analysed data will be used, for example:

Purpose	Classification
Financial accounts	By function - Cost of sales, distribution costs, administrative expenses.
Cost control	By element – materials, labour, other expenses
Cost accounts	By relationship to cost units – direct, indirect
Budgeting, decision making	By behaviour – fixed, variable

3.2 Cost classification by function

For financial accounting purposes costs are split into the following categories:

- **Cost of sales** – also known as production costs. This category could include production labour, materials, supervisor salaries and factory rent.

- **Distribution** – this includes selling and distribution costs such as sales team commission and delivery costs.

- **Administrative costs** – this includes head office costs, IT support, HR support and so on.

- Note that one cost you will meet in the exam is depreciation. This is a measure of how much an asset is wearing out or being used up. The classification will depend on which asset is being depreciated. For example,

- Cost of sales – depreciation on a machine in the production line

- Distribution – depreciation of a delivery van

- Admin – depreciation of a computer in the accounts department

- Classification by function could also be split into **Production** (cost of sales) and **Non-production** costs (distribution and administrative costs) categories.

 Activity 2

George plc makes stationery. Classify the following costs by function in the table below.

Cost	Production	Admin.	Distribution
Purchases of plastic to make pens			
Managing director's bonus			
Depreciation of factory machinery			
Salaries of factory workers			
Insurance of sales team cars			

3.3 Cost classification by element

The simplest classification you will meet in the exam is splitting costs according to element as follows:

- **Materials -** includes raw materials for a manufacturer or alternatively the cost of goods that are to be resold in a retail organisation

- **Labour -** Labour costs can consist of, not only, basic pay but overtime, commissions and bonuses as well.

- **Expenses** – also known as overheads. This includes electricity, depreciation, rent and so on.

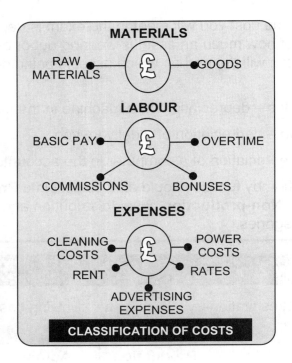

Activity 3

Classify the following costs for a clothes retailer by element in the table below.

Cost	Materials	Labour	Overheads
Designer skirts			
Heating costs			
Depreciation of fixtures and fittings			
Cashier staff salaries			
Carrier bags			

3.4   Cost classification by nature – direct and indirect

To make calculating a cost per unit easier costs are split into the following categories:

- A **direct** cost is an item of cost that is traceable directly to a cost unit.

  For example, the cost of bought-in lights for a car manufacturer.

  The **total of all direct costs** is known as the **prime cost** per unit.

- An **indirect** cost is a cost that either cannot be identified with any one finished unit. Such costs are often referred to as "overheads".

  For example, the rent on a factory.

 Activity 4

Camberwell runs a construction company. Classify the following costs by nature (direct or indirect) in the table below.

Cost	Direct	Indirect
Bricks		
Plant hire for long term contract		
Builders wages		
Accountants wages		

 Activity 5

P Harrington is a golf ball manufacturer . Classify the following costs by nature (direct or indirect) in the table below.

Cost	Direct	Indirect
Machine operators wages		
Supervisors wages		
Resin for golf balls		
Salesmen's salaries		

3.5 Cost classification by behaviour

For budgeting purposes, management needs to be able to predict **how costs will vary with differing levels of activity** (i.e. the number of units being produced).

For example, if a furniture manufacturer expected to produce 1,000 chairs in a particular month, what should he budget for the costs of wood, labour, oil, selling costs, factory heat and light, manager's salaries, etc? How would these costs differ (if at all) if he expected to produce 2,000 chairs?

To make budgeting and forecasting easier, costs are split into the following categories:

- **Variable costs** are those that vary with changes in level of activity. Variable costs are constant per unit of output and increase in direct proportion to activity.

  For example, if you make twice the number of chairs then the amount (and hence the cost) of wood used would double.

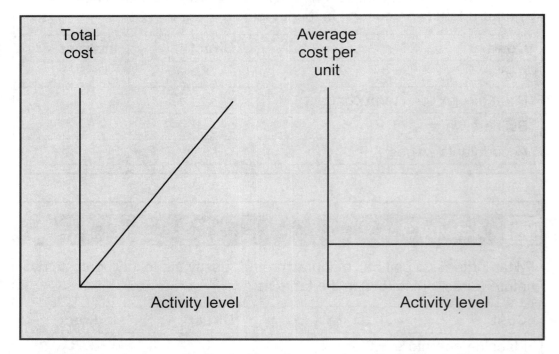

- **Fixed costs** are not affected by changes in activity level. The cost stays constant as activity levels change. This leads to a decrease in the cost per unit of output as activity levels increase.

  For example, the rent on the factory. If the factory is making 10 units of output and the rent is £10,000 then the cost per unit is £100. If the factory then increases production to 1000 units the cost per unit decreases to £10 per unit.

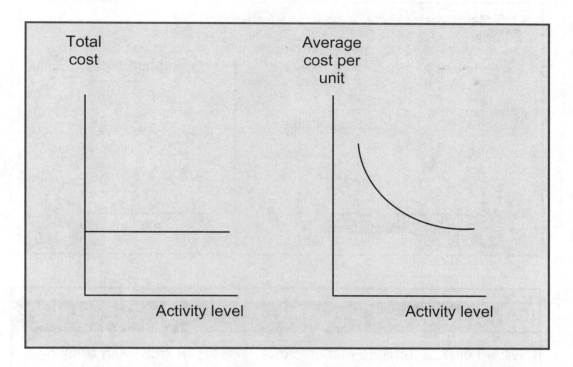

Semi-variable costs are those that have a fixed element and a variable element. For the purpose of budgeting it needs to be possible to separate the fixed and the variable element of a semi-variable cost. This is covered later in the chapter in splitting semi-variable costs.

For example, the cost of electricity for the factory has a fixed element relating to lighting and a variable element relating to power used on the production line.

- **Stepped costs** are costs that remain fixed up to a particular level of activity, but which rise to a higher (fixed) level if activity goes beyond that range.

For example, a firm may pay £40,000 per year to rent a factory in which they can produce up to 1 million units of product per year. However, if demand increases to more than 1 million units a second factory may be required, in which case the cost of factory rent may step up to, say, £80,000 per year and then be constant until we want to make 3 million.

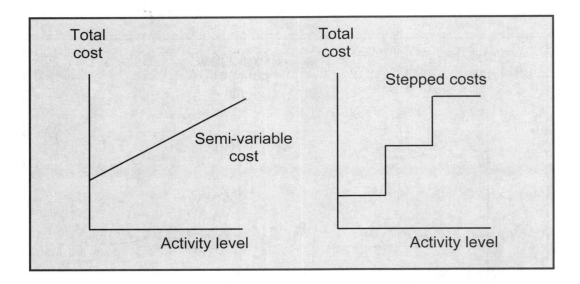

Activity 6

Gilbert plc is a furniture manufacturer. Classify the following costs by their behaviour in the table below.

Cost	Fixed	Variable	Semi-variable
Director's salary			
Wood			
Rent of factory			
Phone bill – includes a line rental			
Factory workers wage			

Activity 7

Which of the following best describes a 'pure' fixed cost?

A cost which:

A   represents a fixed proportion of total costs

B   remains at the same level up to a particular level of output

C   has a direct relationship with output

D   remains at the same level whenever output changes

Activity 8

Identify the following statements as either true or false in the table below.

	True	False
Stepped costs have a fixed and variable element		
Fixed costs vary directly with changes in activity		
Variable costs have a constant cost per unit.		

4 Splitting semi-variable costs

4.1 High/low method

If a semi-variable cost is incurred, it is often necessary to estimate the fixed element and the variable element of the cost for the purposes of budgeting. This can be done using the high/low method.

 Example

A factory has incurred the following power costs in the last six months with different levels of production in each month:

Month	Production in units	Power cost
	£	£
January	20,000	18,000
February	16,000	16,500
March	18,000	17,200
April	24,000	20,500
May	22,000	19,400
June	19,000	17,600

(i) What are the fixed and variable elements of the power cost?
(ii) If production of 30,000 units is anticipated next month, what is the expected power cost?

Solution

Step 1

Find the highest and lowest levels of production and their related power costs.

		Units	Cost £
High	April	24,000	20,500
Low	February	16,000	16,500

Step 2

Find the variable cost element by determining the increased power cost per unit between highest and lowest production levels.

		Units	Cost £
High	April	24,000	20,500
Low	February	16,000	16,500
		8,000	4,000

The power cost has increased by £4,000 for an increase of 8,000 units of production. The variable power cost is therefore:

$$\frac{£4,000}{8,000} = 50 \text{ pence per unit}$$

Step 3

Using either the highest or the lowest production level find the fixed cost element by deducting the variable cost from the total cost.

		£
April	Total cost	20,500
	Variable cost 24,000 × 0.5	12,000
Fixed cost		8,500
February	Total cost	16,500
	Variable cost 16,000 × 0.5	8,000
Fixed cost		8,500

Step 4

Use the fixed cost and variable cost figures to estimate the total power cost if production were 30,000 units.

	£
Variable cost 30,000 × 0.5	15,000
Fixed cost	8,500
Total cost	23,500

When calculating the variable and fixed elements, make sure that you pick the highest and lowest **production levels** and not the highest and lowest **costs**, which will not necessarily be the same.

 Activity 9

The total production cost for making 10,000 units was £12,000 and the total production cost for making 25,000 was £21,000. What is the full production cost for making 40,000 units?

A   6,000

B   24,000

C   30,000

D   72,667

5   Changing activity levels

5.1   Introduction

The behavioural characteristics of the various costs of producing cost units can be used to plan the activities of a business. In particular the distinction between fixed, variable, stepped and semi-variable costs can be used to determine the total cost of production and cost per unit at various activity levels.

Example

A manufacturing business has variable production costs of £3 per unit and fixed costs of £60,000. A further cost is the salary of the factory supervisor of £18,000 per annum. If more than 100,000 units of the product are made then an additional factory supervisor must be employed at the same salary.

What are the total cost of production and the cost per unit at the following production levels:

(i)   60,000 units
(ii)   90,000 units
(iii) 120,000 units?

Solution

	Production level		
	60,000 units £	90,000 units £	120,000 units £
Variable production costs			
60,000 × £3	180,000		
90,000 × £3		270,000	
120,000 × £3			360,000
Fixed costs	60,000	60,000	60,000
Supervisor's salary	18,000	18,000	36,000
Total production cost	258,000	348,000	456,000
Cost per unit	£4.30	£3.87	£3.80

The total costs are made up of both fixed and variable costs but the cost per unit falls as the production quantity increases. This is because the fixed costs are spread over a higher number of units of production.

Activity 10

A manufacturing business has variable production costs of £3 per unit and fixed costs of £50,000. These include rent of £18,000 per annum. If more than 50,000 units of the product are made, then additional floor space must be rented at a cost of £20,000 per annum.

What is the total cost of production and the cost per unit at the 60,000 units:

	Total	Per Unit
A	£230,000	£3.83
B	£250,000	£4.17
C	£268,000	£4.47
D	£88,000	£1.47

6 The cost card

6.1 Cost cards

A cost card is used to show the breakdown of the costs of producing output based on the classification of each cost.

A cost card can be produced for one unit or a planned level of production. The cost card below is an example of a cost card for a planned level of production i.e. in total.

The following chapters are aimed at being able to build up the total or unit cost.

	£
Direct costs	
Direct materials	250,000
Direct labour	120,000
Direct expenses (e.g. royalty payable per unit produced)	10,000
Prime cost *(Total of direct costs)*	380,000
Variable production overheads	15,000
Marginal cost *(total of direct and variable costs)*	395,000
Fixed production overheads	35,000
Absorption cost *(total production cost)*	430,000
Non-production cost (e.g. administration overhead; selling overhead)	20,000
Total cost	450,000

Direct costs are assumed to have **variable** cost behaviours but overheads can be variable, fixed, semi-variable or stepped in behaviour.

7 Cost coding

7.1 Introduction

Cost accounting involves the **detailed analysis of costs** – between cost centres and cost units and between the various types of direct and indirect costs (labour, materials, production overheads, selling, administration, etc).

To facilitate this analysis, a system of **cost coding** is likely to be devised by the organisation. As costs are incurred and recorded within the cost accounts, they will be allocated a code according to the system set out in the costing system manual. For example, the purchases clerk enters the appropriate code on an invoice received for materials before passing it to the data processing department for input. Similarly, timesheets and other documentation used for the initial recording of labour time will generally have a space for coding.

Thus the costs are **analysed accurately and unambiguously at source**, allowing easy production of cost centre and product cost information.

7.2 The structure of cost codes

The simplest form of code structure would be **sequential** where cost, stock and other types of items to be coded are listed and codes allocated in numerical sequence. This is not very useful for sorting and analysis purposes and therefore most coding systems will have some degree of connection between the code and the item it represents.

7.3 Hierarchical systems

The most common structure of cost codes is hierarchical with the detail of the classification of the cost built up from left to right by the individual digits within the code.

For example, the code for the cost of a manager's time spent on a particular client's work in a firm of auditors may be recorded under a code built up as follows:

4	=	Auditing department
42	=	Direct cost (within the auditing department, etc)
421	=	Chargeable employee time
4212	=	Managerial time
42123	=	Correspondence with client
42123ROB15	=	Client

This will allow **analysis of costs** to any level of detail required – by cost centre (using the first digit), by chargeable/non-chargeable time (using the third digit) through to analysis to client (using the last five digits/characters).

Note that the above coding system has used a **mix of numbers and alphabetical characters**. Often codes will be entirely numerical, as these are processed more efficiently on a computer.

7.4 Other code structures

Some items may not form part of a hierarchical structure, but may still have certain characteristics by which they may be grouped (e.g. stock items). An example is a faceted code where each digit or group of digits represents a different characteristic of an item.

> ### Example
>
> An extract from a business's coding manual shows the following:
>
> | | |
> |---|---|
> | Factory cost centre | 02 |
> | Administration cost centre | 05 |
> | Direct materials | 01 |
> | Direct labour | 04 |
>
> What is the cost code for:
>
> (i) direct materials used in the factory?
>
> (ii) direct labour in the administration department?
>
> **Solution**
>
> (i) 0201
>
> (ii) 0504

7.5 Desirable qualities of a coding system

- **Simple to understand and use** – a sophisticated structure will be of little use if used inaccurately.

- **Flexible** – this allows the addition of extra items within the structure or minor changes of classification, etc.

- **Unique and comprehensive** – every item must have one, unique code.

- **Self-checking** – all numerical codes can have a 'check digit' at the end which will be related to the position and size of the digits in the rest of the code by some mathematical formula. This allows the computer to check the accuracy of the code.

If codes have some alphabetical element and if this relates directly to the item being coded, errors may be more easily **spotted by eye**; the solicitor's coding system included the first three letters of the client's name. If this was not compatible with the name written in full on the timesheet, for example, it could easily be spotted.

8 Summary

In this introductory chapter we looked at some of the basic principles and terminology used in cost and management accounting.

Costs can be classified in a variety of different ways for different purposes. The basic classification is into **materials, labour and expenses**, each of which will be dealt with in detail in the following chapters. A further method of classification of costs is between **direct and indirect** costs.

You need to be aware of the difference between **cost units** (individual units of a product or service for which costs can be separately ascertained) and **cost centres** (locations or functions in respect of which costs are accumulated).

For decision-making and budgeting purposes, it is often useful to distinguish costs according to their **behaviour** as production levels change. The basic classifications according to behaviour are **fixed** and **variable** costs although there are also **stepped** costs and **semi-variable** costs. The fixed and variable elements of semi-variable costs can be isolated using the **high/low method**.

 Test your knowledge

Having completed Chapter 1 you should now be able to attempt:

Practice Activities 1, 2, 3, 4 and 5

Answers to chapter activities

Activity 1

Student hours	=	Cost unit
Computer room and library	=	Cost centres

Activity 2

Cost	Production	Admin.	Distribution
Purchases of plastic to make pens	☑		
Managing director's bonus		☑	
Depreciation of factory machinery	☑		
Salaries of factory workers	☑		
Insurance of sales team cars			☑

Activity 3

Cost	Materials	Labour	Overheads
Designer skirts	☑		
Heating costs			☑
Depreciation of fixtures and fittings			☑
Cashier staff salaries		☑	
Carrier bags	☑		

KAPLAN PUBLISHING

Activity 4

Cost	Direct	Indirect
Bricks	☑	
Plant hire for long term contract	☑	
Builders wages	☑	
Accountants wages		☑

Activity 5

Cost	Direct	Indirect
Machine operators wages	☑	
Supervisors wages		☑
Resin for golf balls	☑	
Salesmen's salaries		☑

Activity 6

Cost	Fixed	Variable	Semi-variable
Director's salary	☑		
Wood		☑	
Rent of factory	☑		
Phone bill – includes a line rental			☑
Factory workers wage		☑	

Activity 7

Answer D – Pure fixed costs remain exactly the same in total regardless of the activity level.

Activity 8

	True	False
Stepped costs have a fixed and variable element		☑
Fixed costs vary directly with changes in activity		☑
Variable costs have a constant cost per unit.	☑	

Activity 9

Answer C – see working

	£
Cost of 25,000 units	21,000
Less cost of 10,000 units	12,000
Difference = variable cost of 15,000 units	9,000

Variable cost per unit $= \dfrac{£9,000}{15,000} = 60\text{p each}$

Fixed costs = total cost – variable costs

Fixed costs = £21,000 – £(25,000 × 0.6) = £6,000

Therefore total cost for 40,000

	£
Variable (40,000 × 0.6)	24,000
Fixed	6,000
	30,000

KAPLAN PUBLISHING

Activity 10

Answer B – see working

	60,000 units £
Variable production costs	
60,000 × £3	180,000
Fixed costs	50,000
Additional rentals	20,000
Total production cost	250,000
Cost per unit	£4.17

Material costs

2

Introduction

This chapter considers in more detail materials (stock), the purchasing of materials, the valuation of stock and stock control.

KNOWLEDGE

Explain the purpose of internal reporting and providing accurate information to management in terms of decision making, planning and control (1.1)

Explain the relationship between the various costing and accounting systems within an organisation (1.2)

Identify the most appropriate methods of stock control and valuation (2.1)

SKILLS

Record and analyse costs in accordance with the organisation's costing procedures (1.1)

Analyse cost information for materials, labour and expenses (1.2)

CONTENTS

1 Materials control cycle
2 Materials documentation
3 The stores department
4 The stores record card
5 Pricing issues of raw materials
6 Costs of holding stock
7 Systems of stock control
8 Integrated bookkeeping - materials

1 Materials control cycle

1.1 Introduction

Materials can often form the **largest single item of cost** for a business so it is essential that the material purchased is the most suitable for the intended purpose.

1.2 Control of purchasing

When goods are purchased they must be ordered, received by the stores department, recorded, issued to the manufacturing department that requires them and eventually paid for. This process needs a great deal of paperwork and strict internal controls.

Internal control consists of full documentation and appropriate authorisation of all transactions, movements of materials and of all requisitions, orders, receipts and payments.

If control is to be maintained over purchasing, it is necessary to ensure that:

- only necessary items are purchased

- orders are placed with the most appropriate supplier after considering price and delivery details

- the goods that are actually received are the goods that were ordered and in the correct quantity

- the price paid for the goods is correct (i.e. what was agreed when the order was placed).

To ensure that all of this takes place requires a reliable system of checking and control.

1.3 Overview of procedures

It is useful to have an overview of the purchasing process.

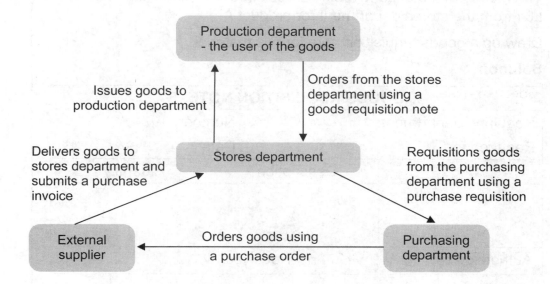

There are many variations of the above system in practice, but it is a fairly typical system and does provide good control over the purchasing and issuing process. Details about the documentation mentioned in the diagram above follows.

 Activity 1 (no feedback)

Your organisation may have a slightly different process to this. See if you can draw a similar diagram illustrating the way your organisation's (or a familiar organisation's) purchasing process works.

2 Materials documentation

2.1 Goods requisition note (also called 'materials requisition')

The user department (e.g. a production department) will notify the stores department that it requires certain goods using a 'goods requisition note'. This note will be authorised by the production manager.

Example

The factory of a company requires 400 litres of a particular oil coded L04 from the stores department for product A.

Draw up a goods requisition note for this material.

Solution

GOODS REQUISITION NOTE		
Requiring department: Factory	Number: 4027	
Required for: Product A	Date: 14 April 20X4	
Code	Description	Quantity
L04	Oil	400 litres
Authorised by: Factory Manager Received by:		

2.2 Purchase requisition

It is important that an organisation **controls** the goods that are ordered from suppliers. Only goods that are genuinely necessary should be ordered. Therefore, before any order for goods is placed, a purchase requisition must be completed.

Each purchase requisition must be **authorised** by the appropriate person. This will usually be the storekeeper or store manager.

When the purchase requisition has been completed it is sent to the purchasing department so that the purchase order is prepared.

 Example

On 15 April the storekeeper of an organisation wishes to order 400 more litres of oil for the machinery. The code for the type of oil that is to be purchased is L04. Delivery is to be made directly to the stores department by 2 May.

Draw up the purchase requisition.

Solution

PURCHASE REQUISITION					
Date: 15 April 20X4				Number: 6843	
Purpose: General machinery maintenance					
Goods requisition note (if any): 4027					
Quantity	Material code	Job code	Delivery details		Purchase order details
			Date	Place	
400 litres	L04	–	2 May 20X4	Stores	
Origination department: Stores					
Authorisation: Storekeeper					

Note that the purchase requisition must have the following elements:

- Be dated.

- Be consecutively numbered.

- Include the purpose for which the materials are required, showing any relevant job code where necessary.

- Include a detailed description of the precise materials required.

- Show when and where the goods are required.

- Include space to record the eventual purchase order details.

- Be authorised by the appropriate person in the department placing the purchase requisition.

2.3 Purchase order

Purchase orders will be placed with suppliers by the purchasing department. The choice of supplier will depend upon the price, delivery promise, quality of goods and past performance.

The person placing the order must first check that the purchase requisition has been authorised by the appropriate person in the organisation.

Once the supplier of the goods has been chosen, the purchase price of the goods must be determined. This will either be from the price list of the supplier or from a special quotation of the price by that supplier. The price agreed will be entered on the purchase order together with details of the goods being ordered.

The purchase order must then be authorised by the appropriate person in the organisation before being dispatched to the supplier.

A copy of the purchase order is sent to the stores department as confirmation of expected delivery. The stores department therefore know that goods are due and can alert appropriate management if they are not received. A copy is also sent to the accounts department to be matched to the supplier's invoice. An example purchase order is shown below.

 Example

From looking at the various possible suppliers' price lists Rowson Supplies Ltd has been chosen. They agree to deliver the oil at a price of £1.50 per litre.

Complete the purchase order in the proforma below.

PURCHASE ORDER					
To:	Number: 81742				
	Date: 15 April 20X4				
	Purchase requisition number: 6843				
Please supply in accordance with attached conditions of purchase.					
Quantity	Description/code	Delivery date	Price £		Per
400 litres	L04	2 May 20X4	1.50		Litre
Your quotation:	£600 (400 litres x £1.50)				
Authorisation:	Purchasing Manager				

2.4 Delivery note

A delivery note is sent by the supplier to the stores with the goods being delivered. This must include full details of the goods being delivered. The delivery note is signed by the person receiving the goods as evidence that the goods arrived.

Example

Rowson Supplies Ltd is delivering 400 litres of oil, code L04, to French Productions Ltd. The delivery takes place on 2 May 20X4 and is in response to a purchase order from French Productions number 81742.

Draw up the delivery note.

Solution

ROWSON SUPPLIES LTD – DELIVERY NOTE		
Delivery to: French Productions Ltd		Date: 2 May 20X4
Purchase order no: 81742		
Delivery note no: D6582		
Please supply in accordance with attached conditions of purchase.		
Quantity	Description	Code
400 litres	Oil	L04
Signed: Storeman		

2.5 Goods received note

When goods are received by the organisation they will be taken to the stores department rather than being delivered directly to the part of the organisation that will use the goods. This enables the receipt of goods to be controlled.

When the goods are received, the stores department will check:

(a) that the goods that arrive agree in **all** detail to those ordered on the purchase order

(b) that the details of the delivery note agree with the actual goods delivered.

When the stores department are satisfied with all of the details of the delivery, the details are recorded on a goods received note (GRN).

Any concerns about the goods being delivered (for example, too few, too many, the wrong colour, the wrong size) should be referred immediately to the appropriate manager before accepting the goods.

The GRN is evidence that the goods that were ordered have been received and therefore should be, and can be, paid for. The GRN will, therefore, be sent to the accounts department to be matched with the supplier's invoice.

As evidence of the actual receipt of the goods the GRN is also used for entering receipts of materials in the stores records.

2.6   Illustration

FRENCH PRODUCTIONS LTD GOODS RECEIVED NOTE			
SUPPLIER: *Rowson Supplies Ltd*		No: GRN 272	
		DATE: *2 May 20X4*	
		PURCHASE ORDER NO: 81742	
Description	Code	Qty	No of packages
Oil	*LO4*	*400 litres*	*1*
Received by: STORES – FINISHING AREA			
Required by: FACTORY			
Accepted by: STORES SUPERVISOR			
QUALITY ASSURANCE			
Inspected by: SIG:			
Qty passed: 400		Qty rejected: Nil	

2.7   Issues to the user department (production department)

The circle is completed when the stores issues the goods to the production department. The goods must agree with the original goods requisition note.

2.8   Purchase invoice

The purchase invoice for goods details the amount that the receiver of the goods must pay for them and the date that payment is due. The purchase invoice might be included when the goods themselves are delivered, or might be sent after delivery.

The person responsible for payment must check that the details of the purchase invoice agree to the goods received note, the delivery note and the purchase order. This is to ensure that:

- what was ordered was received

- what was received is what is being paid for

- the price changed is that agreed.

Once it is certain that the purchase invoice agrees with the goods that were actually received then the invoice can be authorised for payment by the appropriate person in the organisation.

2.9 Illustration

ROWSON SUPPLIES LTD – PURCHASE INVOICE	
To: _Ronson Supplies Ltd_ Date: _2 May 20X4_	
Purchase order no: 81742	
Invoice no: I6582	
	£
For supply and delivery of: 400 litres of oil L04 @ £1.50 per litre Payment due in 30 days	600.00

2.10 Goods returned note

If goods are damaged or are not as ordered, they will be returned to the supplier. A goods returned note will be used, authorised by the stores manager.

When unused materials are returned from user departments to the stores, the transaction will be recorded on a document similar to the materials requisition but usually printed in a different colour. This will be a goods returned note. It will be completed by the user department that is returning the goods and signed by the storekeeper as evidence that the goods were returned to stores.

When the goods are returned the details on the goods returned note must be checked to the actual goods themselves.

2.11 Credit note

If goods have been returned to the supplier, or there is some fault with the invoice (e.g. incorrect price or discount), a credit note will be requested from the supplier.

Activity 2

Which of the following documents would be completed in each situation?

	Material Requisition	Purchase Requisition	Goods received note	Goods returned note
Material returned to stores from production				
Form completed by the stores department detailing stock requirements				
Materials returned to supplier				
Form received with goods on delivery				
Form completed by production detailing stock requirements.				

---

3 The stores department

3.1 Function of the stores department

The stores or stock department is responsible for the receipt, storage, issue and recording of the raw materials used in the production process.

3.2 Receipt of goods

When raw materials are received from suppliers they will normally be delivered to the stores department. The stores personnel must check that the goods delivered are the ones that have been ordered, in the correct quantity, of the correct quality and in good condition using the Goods received note and the purchase requisition or purchase order.

3.3 Storage of materials

Once the materials have been received they must be stored until required by the production departments.

Storage of materials must be appropriate to their type. For example, foodstuffs must be stored at the correct temperature and wood must be stored in dry conditions. Storage should also be laid in such a manner that the correct materials can be accessed easily either manually or by machinery. The cost of storing stock is discussed in a later section.

3.4 Issue of materials

When the production departments require raw materials for production, it is essential that the stores department can provide the correct quantity and quality of materials at the time they are required. This will require careful attention to stock control policies to ensure that the most efficient levels of stocks of raw materials are kept. Stock control policies are discussed in a later section.

3.5 Recording of receipts and issues

In many organisations the stores department is also responsible for the recording of the quantities of raw materials that are received from suppliers and issued to the production departments. This normally takes place on the bin cards or the stores/stock record card.

4 The stores record card

4.1 Stores record card (bin card)

Every line of stock, e.g. component X and material Y, will have a record card showing precisely how much of this item is in stock. Therefore each time a receipt of a material arrives from a supplier then the stores record card must be updated.

A typical stores record card might look like this:

Example

| Material description: | Component X |
| Code: | X100 |

Date	Receipts			Issues			Balance		
	Qty	Unit price £	Total £	Qty	Unit price £	Total £	Qty	Unit price £	Total £

4.2 Stores department entries

In many management accounting systems only the quantity of the materials is entered by the stores department as that is the only information that they have.

4.3 Accounts department entries

Once the stores record card reaches the accounts department then the correct price of the materials, taken from the purchase invoice will be entered.

The stores record card is an important document that helps to control the movement of materials and assess the stock levels of that material.

4.4 Stock ledger account

The accounting for material is dealt with through a stores ledger account (or the material cost account). This is maintained by the accounting department, the physical stock shown on these accounts is reconciled with the stores record card.

Example

Material cost account

	£		£
Balance b/d	81,060	Production/WIP	117,850
Bank/Creditors	71,940	Balance c/d	35,150
	153,000		153,000

5 Pricing issues of raw materials

5.1 Introduction

The cost of materials purchased will normally be derived from suppliers' invoices but, where many purchases have been made at differing prices, a decision has to be taken as to which cost is used when stock is issued to the user department (cost centre).

5.2 Methods of pricing

Various methods exist including:

(a) FIFO (first in, first out)

(b) LIFO (last in, first out)

(c) Weighed average (AVCO)

The choice of method will not only affect the charge to the user department for which the material is required, but also the value of the stock left in stores.

5.3 FIFO, LIFO and AVCO methods

These systems attempt to reflect the movements of individual units in and out of stock under different assumptions.

- **FIFO** – assumes that issues will be made from the oldest stock available, leaving the latest purchases in stock. This means that transfers from stores to production will be made at the oldest prices and the newest prices will be used to value the remaining stock.

  FIFO could be used when products are perishable i.e. milk

- **LIFO** – assumes that issues will be made from the newest stock available, leaving the earliest purchases in stock. This means that transders from stores to production will be made at the newest prices and the older prices will be used to value the remaining stock.

  LIFO could be used when products are not perishable i.e. stationery

- **AVCO** – assumes that the issues into production will be made at an average price. This price is derived from taking the total value of the stock and dividing it by the total units in stock this finding the average price per unit. A new average cost is calculated before each issue to production.

  AVCO could be used when individual units of material are definable e.g. sand at a builders merchants

5.4 The stores record card

As mentioned previous it is usual to record quantities of a stock item (and often stock values as well) on a **stores record card**. One such card is maintained for each different stock item, showing receipts of new stock from suppliers, issues of stock to production, and balance of stock remaining on hand.

Example

Sid makes the following purchases of Component X.

		Quantity	Unit price £	£
Purchases:	10 January	50	1.00	50
	20 January	60	1.10	66
	30 January	40	1.25	50
		150		166

On 25 January Sid issues 70 units for use in production.

On 31 January Sid issues 60 units for use in production.

No stock was held at the beginning of the month.

Calculate the value of closing stock and the cost of stock issued to production using:

(a) a FIFO basis

(b) a LIFO basis

(c) an AVCO basis (round the average price per unit to 2 decimal places)

Solution

(a) **FIFO basis**

Stores Record Card

Material description: Component X
Code: X100

Date	Receipts			Issues			Balance		
	Qty	Unit price £	Total £	Qty	Unit price £	Total £	Qty	Unit price £	Total £
10 Jan	50	1.00	50				50	1.00	50
20 Jan	60	1.10	66				50	1.00	50
							60	1.10	66
							110		116

Date	Qty	Unit price	Total	Qty	Unit price	Total	Qty	Unit price	Total
25 Jan				50	1	50			
				20	1.10	22	40	1.10	44
				70		77			
30 Jan	40	1.25	50				40	1.10	44
							40	1.25	50
							80		94
				40	1.10	44			
				20	1.25	25	20	1.25	25
				60		69	20		25

(b) LIFO basis

Stores Record Card

Material description: Component X

Code: X100

	Receipts			Issues			Balance		
Date	Qty	Unit price £	Total £	Qty	Unit price £	Total £	Qty	Unit price £	Total £
10 Jan	50	1.00	50.00				50	1.00	50.00
20 Jan	60	1.10	66.00				50	1.00	50.00
							60	1.10	66.00
							110		116.00
25 Jan				60	1.10	66.00			
				10	1.00	10.00	40	1.00	40.00
				70		76.00			
30 Jan	40	1.25	50.00				40	1.00	40.00
							40	1.25	50.00
							80		90.00

Date				40	1.25	50.00			
31 Jan				20	1.00	20.00	20	1.00	20.00
				60		70.00	20		20.00

(c)   AVCO basis

Stores Record Card

Material description: Component X

Code: X100

	Receipts			Issues			Balance		
Date	Qty	Unit price £	Total £	Qty	Unit price £	Total £	Qty	Unit price £	Total £
10 Jan	50	1.00	50.00				50	1.00	50.00
20 Jan	60	1.10	66.00				50		50.00
							60		66.00
							110	1.05	116.00
25 Jan							(70)		(73.50)
				70	1.05	73.50			
				70		73.50	40		42.50
30 Jan	40	1.25	50.00				40		42.50
							40		50.00
							80	1.16	92.50
31 Jan							(60)		(69.60)
				60	1.16	69.60			
				60		69.60	20		22.90

Activity 3

Amp plc is a printing company specialising in producing accounting manuals. There is no formal stores accounting system in operation at present.

Complete the following stock entries using:

(a) FIFO

(b) LIFO

(c) AVCO (weighted average cost per unit to two decimal places of a £)

Material:	Paper – Code 1564A
Opening stock:	10,000 sheets – value £3,000

Purchases			Issues	
3 May	4,000 sheets	£1,600	6 May	7,000 sheets
12 May	10,000 sheets	£3,100	15 May	6,000 sheets
25 May	10,000 sheets	£3,200	22 May	7,200 sheets

Stores Record Card FIFO

Material: Paper

Code: 1564A

Date	Details	Receipts		Issues			Stock		
		Sheets	£	Sheets	Price	£	Sheets	Price	£
1.5	Opening stock								
3.5	Receipt								
6.5	Issue								
12.5	Receipt								
15.5	Issue								
22.5	Issue								

Stores Record Card LIFO

Material: Paper

Code: 1564A

Date	Details	Receipts		Issues			Stock		
		Sheets	£	Sheets	Price	£	Sheets	Price	£
1.5	Opening stock								
3.5	Receipt								
6.5	Issue								
12.5	Receipt								
15.5	Issue								
22.5	Issue								

Stores Record Card AVCO

Material: Paper

Code: 1564A

Date	Details	Receipts		Issues			Stock		
		Sheets	£	Sheets	Price	£	Sheets	Price	£
1.5	Opening stock								
3.5	Receipt								
6.5	Issue								
12.5	Receipt								
15.5	Issue								
22.5	Issue								

5.5 Features of the different methods

FIFO is fairly easy to understand. FIFO has the following features:

- In times of rapidly increasing prices, material may be issued at an early and unrealistically low price, resulting in the particular job showing an unusually large profit.

- Two jobs started on the same day may show a different cost for the same quantity of the same material.

- In times of rapidly increasing prices FIFO will give a higher profit figure than LIFO or AVCO.

LIFO is also fairly simple to follow. LIFO has the following features:

- Closing stocks will be shown at the earliest prices which means that in times of rapidly increasing or decreasing prices, the stock figure bears little resemblance to the current cost of replacement

- As for FIFO, two jobs started on the same day may show a different cost for the same quantity of the same material.

- The LIFO method uses the latest prices for issues to production and therefore the cost obtained is more likely to be in line with other costs and selling prices.

- In times of rapidly increasing prices LIFO will give a lower profit figure than FIFO and AVCO.

AVCO is a compromise on valuation of stock and issues and the average price rarely reflects the actual purchase price of the material.

5.6 Stock valuation method and profit

As stated above FIFO will return a higher profit than LIFO if prices are rapidly increasing.

 Example

Charlie has the following extract from there stock card and was wondering which method of stock valuation would give him the highest profit.

1 July Received 100 units at £10 per unit

2 July Received 100 units at £11 per unit

3 July Issued 150 units to production.

There is no opening stock.

Using LIFO the issues to production would be valued at £1600 (100 @ £11 and 50 @ £10) and the closing inventory would be valued at £500 (50 @ £10)

Using FIFO the issues to production would be valued at £1550 (100 @ £10 and 50 @ £11) and the closing inventory would be valued at £550 (50 @ £11)

If these are put into the cost of sales calculation in an income statement you can see what the impact on profit is.

LIFO		FIFO	
Opening stock	0	Opening stock	0
Production	1,600	Production	1,550
Closing stock	(500)	Closing stock	(550)
Cost of sales	1,100	Cost of sales	1,000

FIFO has a lower cost of sales than LIFO, therefore less cost meaning a higher profit.

 Activity 4

If raw material prices are subject to inflation, which method of valuing stocks will give the lowest profit?

A   FIFO

B   LIFO

C   AVCO

6   Cost of holding stock

6.1   Introduction

Most businesses, whatever their size, will be concerned with the problem of which items to have in stock and how much of each item should be kept.

KAPLAN PUBLISHING

6.2   Functions of stock

The principal reasons why a business needs to hold stock are as follows:

(a)   It acts as a buffer in times when there is an unusually high rate of consumption.

(b)   It enables the business to take advantage of quantity discounts by buying in bulk.

(c)   The business can take advantage of seasonal and other price fluctuations (e.g. buying coal in the summer when it is cheaper).

(d)   Any delay in production caused by lack of parts is kept to a minimum, so production processes will flow smoothly and efficiently.

(e)   It may be necessary to hold stock for a technical reason: for example, whisky must be matured.

6.4   Costs of holding stock

Irrespective of the nature of the business, a certain amount of stock will need to be held.

However, **holding stock costs money** and the principal 'trade-off' in a stockholding situation is between the costs of acquiring and storing stocks on the one hand and the level of service that the company wishes to provide on the other.

The **total cost of having stock** consists of the following:

(a)   **Purchase price** (as affected by discounts).

(b)   **Holding costs**:

    (i)   the opportunity cost of capital tied up

    (ii)   insurance

    (iii)   deterioration

    (iv)   obsolescence

    (v)   damage and pilferage

    (vi)   warehouse upkeep

    (vii)   stores labour and administration costs.

(c)   **Ordering costs**:

    (i)   clerical and administrative expenses

    (ii)   transport costs.

    Note, if goods are produced internally, the set-up costs for each production run are equivalent to the re-order costs.

(d) **Stock-out costs** (items of required stock are not available):

    (i)   loss of sales, therefore lost contribution

    (ii)   long-term damage to the business through loss of goodwill

    (iii) production stoppages caused by a shortage of raw materials

    (iv) extra costs caused by the need for emergency orders.

(e) **Stock recording systems costs**:

    (i)   maintaining the stores record card

6.6 Disadvantages of low stock levels

- To keep the holding costs low it may be possible to reduce the volume of stock that is kept but this can cause some problems:

- Customer demand cannot always be satisfied; this may lead to loss of business if customers become dissatisfied.

- In order to fulfil commitments to important customers, costly emergency procedures (e.g. special production runs) may become necessary in an attempt to maintain customer goodwill.

- It will be necessary to place replenishment orders more frequently than if higher stocks were held, in order to maintain a reasonable service. This will result in higher ordering costs being incurred.

6.7 Disadvantages of high stock levels

- To reduce the problems mentioned above management may consider holding high levels of stock but again this can have issues:

- Storage or holding costs are very high; such costs will usually include rates, rent, labour, heating, deterioration, etc.

- The cost of the capital tied up in stocks, i.e. the cash spent to buy the stock is not available to pay other bills.

- If the stored product becomes obsolete, a large stockholding of that item could, at worst, represent a large capital investment in an unsaleable product whose cash value is only that of scrap.

- If a great deal of capital is invested in stocks, there will be proportionately less money available for other requirements such as improvement of existing production facilities, or the introduction of new products.

- When a high stock level of a raw material is held, a sudden drop in the market price of that material represents a cash loss to the business for having bought at the higher price. It follows that it would seem sensible to hold higher stocks during an inflationary period and lower stocks during a period of deflation.

7 Systems of stock control

7.1 Stock control

Stock control is 'the method of ensuring that the right **quantity** of the right quality of the relevant stock is available at the right **time** and right **place**.

Stock control is maintained through the use of the stock record card and by carrying out stock checks on a regular basis.

7.2 Terminology

The following terms will be used in this section and the next:

Lead time	The time between an order for goods being placed and the receipt of that order.
Usage	The quantity of items required for sale (in the case of goods for resale) or production (in the case of components or raw materials) in a given period.
Re-order level	The quantity of stock in hand at the time when a new order is placed.
Re-order quantity	The quantity of stock ordered.
Economic order quantity (EOQ)	The most economic quantity of stock to be ordered/produced to minimise the total of the inventory costs
Buffer stock	Stock held to cover variations in: – lead time – demand during the lead time.

7.3 Stock control levels

Many stock control systems will incorporate some or all of four stock control levels that assist in keeping costs of stockholding and ordering down, whilst minimising the chances of stock-outs. The four control levels are:

- re-order level – the level to which the stock will be allowed to fall before an order is placed

- economic order quantity (EOQ) – the most economic quantity of stock to be ordered to minimise the total of the cost having stock.

- maximum stock level – the highest quantity of stock that should be held

- minimum stock level – the lowest quantity of stock that should be held (also known as buffer stock)

7.4 Re-order level

This level will be determined with reference to the time it will take to receive the order (the lead time) and the possible stock requirements during that time.

If it is possible to estimate the **maximum possible lead time** and the **maximum usage rate**, then a 'safe' re-order level, that will almost certainly avoid stock-outs, will be given by:

Re-order level = Maximum usage × Maximum lead time

7.5 Economic order quantity (EOQ)

Once the re-order level is reached, an order will be placed. The size of the order will affect:

(a) average stock levels (the larger the order, the higher the stock levels will be throughout the year)

(b) frequency of orders placed in the year (the larger the order, the longer it will take for stocks to fall to the re-order level, and thus the fewer the orders placed in the year).

Increasing the order size will have two conflicting effects on costs: increased holding costs through higher stock levels and decreased re-ordering costs due to fewer orders placed in the year.

Under certain 'ideal' conditions (including constant rates of usage and constant lead times) a mathematical model can be used to determine the optimum (economic) order quantity (EOQ) that will minimise the total of these two costs – see graph below.

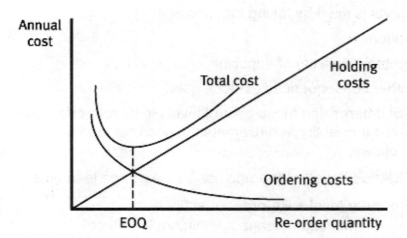

The formula for the economic order quantity is:

$$EOQ = \sqrt{\frac{2 \times C_o \times D}{C_h}}$$

where: C_o = cost of placing each order (note this is not the cost of the materials purchased but the administrative cost of placing the order).

D = annual demand/usage in units

C_h = cost of holding **one** unit of stock for **one** year

7.6 Maximum and minimum stock levels

Many stock systems will also incorporate maximum and minimum stock 'warning' levels, above or below which (respectively) stock should not be allowed to rise/fall.

In practice, the maximum stock level is fixed by taking into account:

(a)   rate of consumption of the material

(b)   time needed to obtain new supplies

(c)   financial considerations due to high stocks tying up capital

(d)   storage space with regard to the provision of space and maintenance costs

(e)   extent to which price fluctuates

(f) risks of changing specifications

(g) possibility of loss by evaporation, deterioration, etc

(h) seasonal considerations as to both price and availability

(i) economic order quantities.

The minimum stock level is fixed by taking into account:

(a) rate of consumption

(b) time needed to obtain delivery of supplies

(c) the costs and other consequences of stock-outs.

A simplified method of determining these control levels is by reference to the re-order level, re-order quantity and estimates of possible lead times and usage rates, as follows:

Minimum level = Re-order level – (Average usage × Average lead time)

Maximum level = Re-order level + Re-order quantity –
(Minimum usage × Minimum lead time)

If at any time stocks **fall below the minimum level**, this is a warning that **usage or lead time are above average**. Thus the storekeeper will need to keep an eye on stock levels and be prepared to place an emergency order if stocks get too low.

If stocks **rise above the maximum level** then **usage or lead time have actually been lower** than the expected minimum. If it is usage, this may indicate a general decline in the demand for the stock and the order quantity (and possibly the re-order level) should be reviewed to avoid holding excess stock with associated holding costs.

 Example

The demand for a particular product is expected to vary between 10 and 50 per day, with an average of 25. Lead time is, on average, 5 days, although it has been as short as 3 days and as long as 10 days.

Each time an order is placed, administrative costs of £15 are incurred and one unit of stock held for one year incurs £0.10 of holding costs.

The company operates a 300-day year.

Calculate the four control levels.

Solution

Re-order level	=	Maximum usage × Maximum lead time
	=	50 per day × 10 days = 500 units

$$\text{EOQ} = \sqrt{\frac{2 \times C_o \times D}{C_h}}$$

$$\text{EOQ} = \sqrt{\frac{[2 \times £15 \times 7,500 \, (W)]}{£0.10}} = 1,500 \text{ units}$$

Minimum level	=	Re-order level – (Average usage × Average lead time)
	=	500 – (25 per day × 5 days) = 375 units
Maximum level	=	Re-order level + EOQ – (Minimum usage × Minimum lead time)
	=	500 + 1,500 – (10 per day × 3 days) = 1,970 units

Working

Annual demand D = days in year × average usage per day

$$D = 300 \times 25 = 7,500$$

Activity 5

Given below is information about one stock line that a business holds:

	Lowest	Average	Highest
Daily usage (units)	15	20	25
Lead time	2	5	8

The business operates for 250 days a year.

The cost of placing each order is £20 and it costs £0.20 to hold an item of stock for one year.

Calculate:

(i)   the re-order level

(ii)   the economic order quantity

(iii)   the maximum stock level

(iv)   the minimum stock level.

7.7   Stock control systems

There are two main types of stock control systems:

(a)   the re-order level (two-bin) system

(b)   the periodic (cyclical) review system

7.8   Re-order level system

In a **re-order level system**, a replenishment order of fixed size is placed when the stock level falls to the fixed re-order level. Thus a **fixed quantity** is ordered at **variable intervals of time**. This is the most common system used.

The most common practical implementation of the basic re-order level system is the two-bin system. Here, two bins of the stock item are used and a replenishment order is placed when the first bin becomes empty; stock is then drawn from the second bin until the order is received. When the order arrives, the second bin is filled up to its original level and the remainder goes into the first (empty) bin. Thus the amount of stock held in the second bin gives the re-order level.

7.9   Periodic review system

In a **periodic review system**, the stock levels are reviewed at fixed points in time, when the quantity to be ordered is decided. By this method **variable quantities** are ordered at **fixed time intervals**.

Although this may increase the chances of a stock-out (between review times), it has the advantage of being easier to plan the scheduling of stock-counts and orders in advance.

8 Integrated bookkeeping - materials

8.1 Introduction

The costs of a business have to be recorded in a bookkeeping system. Many businesses use an **intergrated bookkeeping system** where the ledger accounts kept provide the necessary **information for both costing and financial accounting**.

[handwritten note: Re-order quantity = EOQ. material at cost. Account at Store Deput. record the raw material]

... account is where the movement of the costs associated ...

Example

Materials cost account

	£		£
Opening balance (1)		Issues to production (4)	
Purchases (2)		Returns to suppliers (5)	
Returns to stores (3)		Production overheads (6)	
		Profit and Loss (7)	
		Closing balance (8)	
	____		____
	____		____

(1) The **opening balance** of materials held in stores at the beginning of a period is shown as a **debit** in the material cost account.

(2) Materials **purchased** on credit are **debited** to the material cost account. Materials purchased for cash would also be a debit

(3) Materials **returned to stores** cause stock to increase and so are **debited** to the material inventory account

(4) **Direct materials** used in production are transferred to the **production** account, which is also known as the **Work-In-Progress**. The is recorded by crediting the material inventory account

(5) Materials **returned to suppliers** cause stock levels to fall and are therefore '**credited**' out of the materials cost account

(6) **Indirect materials** are not a direct cost of manufacture and are treated as **overheads**. They are therefore transferred to the production overhead account by way of a **credit** to the materials cost account

(7) Any material **write-offs** are '**credited** out' of the material cost account and transferred to the profit and loss where they are written off

(8) The **balancing figure** on the materials cost account is the **closing balance** of material stock at the end of a period. It is also the opening balance at the beginning of the next period

---

 Activity 6

What are the correct journal entries the following accounting transactions:

1   Receipt of material into stores paying on credit:

    A   Dr Bank, Cr Materials

    B   Dr Trade Creditors Control, Cr Materials

    C   Dr Materials, Cr Bank

    D   Dr Materials, Cr Trade Creditors Control

2   Issue of material from stock to production.

    A   Dr Bank, Cr Materials

    B   Dr Materials, Cr Bank

    C   Dr Materials, Cr Production

    D   Dr Production, Cr Materials

3   Receipt of material into stores paying immediately by BACS.

    A   Dr Bank, Cr Materials

    B   Dr Trade Creditors Control, Cr Materials

    C   Dr Materials, Cr Bank

    D   Dr Materials, Cr Trade Creditors Control

4   Return of material from production to stores.

    A   Dr Materials, Cr Bank

    B   Dr Materials, Cr Trade Creditors Control

    C   Dr Materials, Cr Production

    D   Dr Production, Cr Materials

9 Summary

Pricing issues of raw materials and valuing stocks are two of the most important techniques that you need to know about in the topic of materials. We have looked at three main methods of pricing issues and valuing stocks: FIFO, LIFO, and Weighted Average Cost. A common examination task is to ask you to record receipts and issues of materials onto a stores ledger card using one of these methods.

We have also looked at the **documents** involved in the process of purchasing materials and the different stock control systems (re-order level (two-bin) system, periodic review system and the just-in-time system).

Another important part of the topic of materials is that of **stock control** levels – these assist in keeping the costs of stockholding and stock ordering at a minimum, whilst minimising stock-outs at the same time. Make sure that you can calculate the re-order level, the EOQ, the maximum stock level and the minimum stock level

 Test your knowledge

Having completed Chapter 2 you should now be able to attempt:

Practice Activities 6, 7, 8, 9, 10, 11 and 12

Answers to chapter activities

 Activity 1

There is no correct answer to this question. All organisations will have a slightly different approach to the purchasing process.

 Activity 2

Which of the following documents would be completed in each situation?

	Materials Requisition	Purchase Requisition	Goods received note	Goods returned note
Material returned to stores from production				☑
Form completed by the stores department detailing stock requirements		☑		
Materials returned to supplier				☑
Form received with goods on delivery			☑	
Form completed by production detailing stock requirements.	☑			

Activity 3

Stores Record Card FIFO

Material: Paper
Code: 1564A

Date	Details	Receipts Sheets	£	Issues Sheets	Price	£	Stock Sheets	Price	£
1.5	Opening stock						10,000	0.30	3,000
3.5	Receipt	4,000	1,540				10,000	0.30	3,000
							4,000	0.40	1,600
							14000		4600
6.5	Issue						3,000	0.30	900
				7,000	0,30	2100	4000	0.40	1600
				7,000		2100	7000		2500
12.5	Receipt	10,000	3,100				3,000	0.30	900
							4000	0.40	1600
							10,000	0.31	3,100
							17000		5600
15.5	Issue			3,000	0.30	900	1,000	0.40	400
				3,000	0.40	1200	10,000	0.31	3100
				6,000		2100	11,000		3500
22.5	Issue			1,000	0.40	400			
				6,200	0.31	1,922	3,800	0.31	1,178
				7,200		2,322	3,800		1,178

Stores Record Card LIFO

Material: Paper
Code: 1564A

Date	Details	Receipts Sheets	£	Issues Sheets	Price	£	Stock Sheets	Price	£
1.5	Opening stock						10,000	0.30	3,000
3.5	Receipt	4,000	1,600				10,000	0.30	3,000
							4,000	0.40	1,600
							14000		4600
6.5	Issue			4,000	0.40	1,600			
				3,000	0,30	900	7,000	0.30	2,100
				7,000		2,500	7,000		2,100
12.5	Receipt	10,000	3,100				7,000	0.30	2,100
							10,000	0.31	3,100
							17,000		5,200
15.5	Issue						7,000	0.30	2100
				6,000	0.31	1860	4,000	0.31	1240
				6,000		2100	11,000		3340

Date	Details	Receipts Sheets	£	Issues Sheets	Price	£	Stock Sheets	Price	£
22.5	Issue			4,000	0.31	1240			
				3,200	0.30	960	3,800	0.30	1,140
				7,200		2,200	3,800		1,140

Stores Record Card AVCO

Material: Paper

Code: 1564A

Date	Details	Receipts		Issues			Stock		
		Sheets	£	Sheets	Price	£	Sheets	Price	£
1.5	Opening stock						10,000		3,000
3.5	Receipt	4,000	1,600				14,000	0.33	4,600
6.5	Issue			7,000	0.33	2,310	7,000		2,290
12.5	Receipt	10,000	3,100				17,000	0.32	5,390
15.5	Issue			6,000	0.32	1,920	11,000		3,470
22.5	Issue			7,200	0.32	2,304	3,800		1,166

 Activity 4

Answer B LIFO

 Activity 5

(i) Re-order level = Maximum usage × Maximum lead time

= 25 units × 8 days

= 200 units

(ii) EOQ = $\sqrt{\dfrac{2 \times C \times D}{h}}$

= $\sqrt{\dfrac{2 \times £20 \times 20 \times 250)}{0.2}}$

= 1,000 units

(iii) Maximum stock level = Re-order level + EOQ – (Minimum usage × Minimum lead time)

= 200 + 1,000 – (15 × 2)

= 1,170 units

(iv) Minimum stock level = Re-order level –
                              (Average usage × Average lead time)
                           = 200 – (20 × 5)
                           = 100 units

 Activity 6

What are the correct journal entries the following accounting transactions:

1. Receipt of material into stores paying on credit:
    D   Dr Materials, Cr Trade Creditors Control

2. Issue of material from stores to production:
    D   Dr Production, Cr Materials

3. Receipt of material into stores paying immediately by BACS:
    C   Dr Materials, Cr Bank

4. Return of material from production to stores.
    C   Dr Materials, Cr Production

Labour costs

Introduction

Labour is a **major cost** for many organisations. The cost of labour will depend on the remuneration (payment) system used by an organisation for example: annual salary, hourly rates and overtime or piecework payments.

KNOWLEDGE

Explain the purpose of internal reporting and providing accurate information to management in terms of decision making, planning and control (1.1)

Explain the relationship between the various costing and accounting systems within an organisation (1.2)

SKILLS

Record and analyse costs in accordance with the organisation's costing procedures (1.1)

Analyse cost information for materials, labour and expenses (1.2)

CONTENTS

1 Employee records
2 Remuneration systems
3 Direct and indirect labour costs
4 Integrated bookkeeping – Labour

1 Employee records

1.1 Attendance records

In most businesses, **records** are needed of the time spent by each employee in the workplace (attendance time) and time spent on the operations, processes, products or services whilst there (job time). Such timekeeping provides basic data for statutory records, payroll preparation, ascertainment and control of labour costs of an operation or product, overhead distribution (where based on wages or labour hours) and statistical analysis of labour records for determining productivity.

Attendance may be recorded by using a **register**, in which employees note their times of arrival and departure, or by means of a **time recording clock** which stamps the times on a card inserted by each employee. Alternatively, employees may be required to submit periodic **timesheets** showing the amounts of normal and overtime work; these may also include job times.

1.2 Personnel record details

When an employee joins an organisation it is necessary to record a number of details about him and the details of his job and pay. The personnel department completes this in the individual employee's personnel record.

The type of details that might be kept about an employee are as follows:

- Full name, address and date of birth.

- Personal details such as marital status and emergency contact name and address.

- National Insurance number.

- Previous employment history.

- Educational details.

- Professional qualifications.

- Date of joining organisation

- Employee number or code.

- Clock number issued.

- Job title and department.

- Rate of pay agreed.

- Holiday details agreed.

- Bank details if salary is to be paid directly into bank account.

- Amendments to any of the details above (such as increases in agreed rates of pay).

- Date of termination of employment (when this takes place) and reasons for leaving.

 Example

Jonathan Minor started to be employed by your organisation on 1 July 2001 as an engineer in the maintenance department of the organisation. He was born on 22 January 1983 and this is his first job after training at college for an HND in engineering.

His employee code and clock number are M36084 and his agreed rate of pay is £375.60 per week. He is to be paid in cash.
Complete the employee personnel record for Jonathan.

Solution

PERSONNEL RECORD CARD			
PERSONAL DETAILS			**EMPLOYMENT DETAILS**
Surname: MINOR Other names: JONATHAN	Address: 24 Hill St Reading	Emergency contact: Jane MINOR 24 Hill St Reading	**Previous Employment History**
Date of birth: 22/1/83	Nationality: British	Sex: M	Employer: Date:
Marital status: Single		Dependents: None	(1)
National Insurance Number: WE 22 41 79 J9			(2)
EDUCATIONAL DETAILS			(3)
			(4)
Degree: –		Btec/HND: Engineering	**TRAINING DETAILS**
A Levels: 2	O Levels: 0	GCSE: 7	CSEs: 0	Course attended: Date:
University attended:		–	
College attended:		Reading	
Schools attended (with dates):		Reading High (1994 – 1999) Reading Junior (1987 – 1994)	

JOB DETAILS			OTHER DETAILS
Date of joining: 1/7/01	Clock number:	M36084	Bank account:
Job title: Engineer	Department:	Maintenance	
Rate of pay:	Overtime:	1½ times basic	Date of termination:
Date £	Holiday:	15 days	
1/7/01 375.60 pw	Pension Scheme:		Reason for leaving:
	Joined:	1/7/01	

1.3   Attendance records

In most businesses, **records** are needed of the time spent by each employee in the workplace (attendance time) and time spent on the operations, processes, products or services whilst there (job time). Such timekeeping provides basic data for statutory records, payroll preparation, ascertainment and control of labour costs of an operation or product, overhead distribution (where based on wages or labour hours) and statistical analysis of labour records for determining productivity.

Attendance may be recorded by using a **register**, in which employees note their times of arrival and departure, or by means of a **time recording clock** which stamps the times on a card inserted by each employee. Alternatively, employees may be required to submit periodic **timesheets** showing the amounts of normal and overtime work; these may also include job times.

1.4   Holiday records

An employee will usually have an agreed number of days holiday per year. This will usually be paid holiday for salaried employees but may well be unpaid for employees paid by results or on time rates.

It is important for the employer to keep a record of the number of holiday days taken by the employee to ensure that the agreed number per year is not exceeded.

1.5   Sickness records

The organisation will have its own policies regarding payment for sick leave as well as legal requirements for statutory sick pay. Therefore, it will be necessary to keep a record of the number of days of sick leave each year for each employee.

1.6   Other periods of absence

A record will need to be kept of any other periods of absence by an employee. These might be perfectly genuine such as jury service or training courses or alternatively unexplained periods of absence that must be investigated.

1.7 Source of information

Information about an employee's attendance will come from various sources such as clock cards, time sheets and cost cards.

1.8 Clock cards

A **clock card** is a document on which is recorded the starting and finishing time of an employee for ascertaining total actual attendance time

A clock card is usually some form of electronic or computerised recording system whereby when the employee's clock card is entered into the machine the time is recorded. This will give the starting and finishing time for the day and also in some systems break times taken as well.

Clock cards are used as a source document in the calculation of the employee's earnings.

Example

Example of a clock card

Works number:			Name:		
		Lunch			
Week ending	In	Out	In	Out	Hours
Monday					
Tuesday					
Wednesday					
Thursday					
Friday					
Saturday					
Sunday					
FOREMAN'S SIGNATURE:					

1.9 Daily timesheets

One of these sheets is filled in by each employee (to indicate the time spent by them on each job) and passed to the cost office each day. The total time on the timesheet should correspond to the time shown on the attendance record. Times are recorded daily meaning there is less risk of times being forgotten or manipulated, but these timesheets create a considerable volume of paperwork.

Below is an illustration of a daily timesheet.

 Example

Name:	Frank Smith			Date:		11/6/X5
Clock number:	3			Week number:	31	

Job order number	Description	Time		Hours worked	Rate	£
		Start	Finish			
349	Servicing Ford Ka Y625 AAB	9.00	11.05	2.05		
372	Repair to Range Rover TC03 XYZ	11.05	16.30	4.25		

Signed:	F Smith	Certified:	A Foreman	Office ref:

1.10 Weekly timesheets

These are similar to daily timesheets but they are passed to the cost office at the end of the week instead of every day (although entries should be made daily in order to avoid error). Weekly timesheets are particularly suitable where there are few job changes in the course of a week.

Activity 1

Below is the weekly timesheet for Thomas Yung (employee number Y4791), who is paid as follows:

- For a basic six-hour shift every day from Monday to Friday - basic pay.

- For any overtime in excess of the basic six hours, on any day from Monday to Friday - the extra hours are paid at time-and-a-half.

- For three contracted hours each Saturday morning - basic pay.

- For any hours in excess of three hours on Saturday - the extra hours are paid at double time.

- For any hours worked on Sunday - paid at double time

Complete the columns headed Basic pay, Overtime premium and Total pay. Zero figures should be entered in cells where appropriate.

Employee's weekly timesheet for week ending 12 December						
Name: Thomas Yung				**Cost centre:** Machining		
Employee number: Y4791				**Basic Pay per hour:** £12		
	Hours spent on:		Notes	Basic pay £	Overtime premium £	Total pay £
	Production	Indirect work				
Monday	6	2	1 - 3pm cleaning machinery			
Tuesday	2	4	9am – 1pm training course			
Wednesday	8					
Thursday	6					
Friday	6	1	2-3pm health and safety training			
Saturday	6					
Sunday	3					
Total	37	7				

2 Remuneration systems

Remuneration 报酬. 酬劳.
remunerate. 酬劳.

overtime premium. = 5 × 0.5 × 8.20
overtime x.
5 Hrs Normal rate £8.20
overtime paid at 1.5 time.

2.1 Introduction

Employees in a business will be remunerated or paid for the work that they do. There are a variety of different ways in which this payment is calculated. The main systems of remuneration are:

- annual salaries
- hourly rates of pay and overtime payments
- piecework payments
- bonus schemes.

Different types of employees within a business may well be paid according to different systems depending upon which is the most appropriate for the type of work that they perform.

2.2 Annual salaries

Annual salaries tend to be paid to management and non-production staff such as administrators, secretaries, accounts staff, etc. The annual salary is simply divided by the 12 months in the year and that is the amount of gross pay for that employee for the month.

 Example

The sales manager of a business has an annual salary of £30,000. What is the gross amount of his pay each month?

Solution

Monthly gross pay =   £30,000/12

             =   £2,500

2.3 Hourly rates and overtime payments

Many production and manual workers will be paid for every hour that they work. Normally hourly paid workers will have a standard number of hours that they work each week. If they work for more than this number of hours then they will have worked overtime, which will usually be paid more than the basic hourly rate.

The overtime payment is the total amount paid the extra hours worked. The overtime premium is the extra per hour that is paid to an employee for the extra time that is worked.

Example

An employee works for a standard week of 40 hours at an hourly rate of pay of £8.20. Any overtime hours are paid at time and a half.

In one week he works for 45 hours.

(i)   What is his gross pay?

(ii)   What is his overtime payment?

(iii)   What is his overtime premium?

Solution

(i)

		£
Basic hours 40 × £8.20		328.00
Overtime 5 × (£8.20 × 1.5)		61.50
		————
Gross pay		389.50
		————

(ii)   Overtime payment — £61.50

(iii)   Overtime premium
        5 × (£8.20 × 0.5) — = £20.50

Activity 2

An employee's basic week is 40 hours at a rate of pay of £5 per hour. Overtime is paid at 'time and a half'. What is the wage cost of this employee if he works for 45 hours in a week?

A   £225.00

B   £237.50

C   £300.00

D   £337.50

2.4   Piecework payments

Piecework rates occur where a fixed constant amount is paid per unit of output. The fixed rate will often be based upon the standard (expected) time per unit. This method is an example of 'payment by results'.

Example

Graeme MacHue works in the Scottish Highlands producing carved wooden animals for a small company supplying the tourist market. In week 26 his production was:

	Standard time allowed/unit
6 Stags	2.0 hours
5 Otters	1.5 hours
12 Owls	1.0 hour
6 Golden Eagles	2.0 hours

He is paid £5 per standard hour of production (irrespective of actual time worked).

What are his earnings for week 26?

Solution

		£
Stags	6 × 2 × £5	60.00
Otters	5 × 1.5 × £5	37.50
Owls	12 × 1 × £5	60.00
Golden Eagles	6 × 2 × £5	60.00
		―――――
		217.50
		―――――

Advantages of the piecework system

- It produces a constant labour cost per unit.

- It **encourages efficient work** – an employee taking more than the standard time per unit will only be paid for the standard time. In order for this to motivate, the employee must accept the standard as fair.

To increase motivation, a **differential piecework system** may be implemented, whereby the piece rate is increased for higher output levels.

Disadvantages of the piecework system

- Employees **lack security of income**, so may become demotivated.

- The employee can be **penalised** for low levels of production due to factors that are outside his/her control (e.g. machine breakdown)

2.5 Guaranteed minimum payment

To overcome these disadvantages, the **straight piecework rate** may be accompanied by a **guaranteed minimum payment** (weekly or daily).

Example

Standard rate per hour	=	£4.50
Guaranteed minimum per week	=	35 hours

Actual production: 10 units @ 3 hours per unit. Calculate the weekly pay.

Solution

Standard hours	=	10 × 3 = 30 hours
Pay	=	30 × £4.50 = £135
Subject to guaranteed minimum pay	=	35 × £4.50 = £157.50
Therefore weekly pay	=	£157.50

Activity 3

A company operates a piecework system of remuneration. Employees must work for a minimum of 40 hours per week. Joe produces the following output for a particular week:

Product	Quantity	Standard time per item (hours)	Total actual time (hours)
Gaskets	50	0.2	9
Drive belts	200	0.06	14
Sprockets	100	0.1	12
Gears	10	0.7	6
			41

He is paid £6.20 per standard hour worked. What are his earnings for the week?

A £129.60

B £254.20

C £241.80

D £498.48

Activity 4

Jones is paid £3.00 for every unit that he produces but he has a guaranteed wage of £28.00 per eight-hour day. In a particular week he produces the following number of units:

Monday	12 units
Tuesday	14 units
Wednesday	9 units
Thursday	14 units
Friday	8 units

Jones's wages for the week are:

A £176

B £175

C £172

D £171

 Activity 5

Continuing with the example of Jones above, what would be his weekly wage if the guarantee were for £140 per week rather than £28 per day?

A £176

B £175

C £172

D £171

2.6 Bonus schemes

Bonus schemes are a compromise between a day rate and a piecework system. Earnings will comprise:

(a) a day rate amount, based on hours worked, and

(b) a bonus based on quantity produced (usually above a certain standard) or on time saved in relation to standard time allowance for the output achieved.

KAPLAN PUBLISHING

Example

On a particular day, Fred worked for 8.5 hours, producing 15 units. The standard time allowance for each unit is 40 minutes. Fred's basic hourly rate is £4.50 and he is paid a bonus for time saved from standard at 60% of his basic hourly rate.

Calculate Fred's pay for the day.

Solution

		£
Day rate = 8.5 × £4.50		38.25
Bonus		
Standard time 15 × 40/60	10 hours	
Actual time	8.5 hours	
	———	
Time saved	1.5 hours	
	———	
Bonus = 1.5 × £4.50 × 60%		4.05
		———
Total		42.3
		———

2.7 Group bonus schemes

In the case of, for example, an assembly line, where it is impossible for an individual worker on the line to increase productivity without the others also doing so, a group bonus scheme may be used. The bonus is calculated by reference to the output of the group and split between the members of the group (often equally).

 Example

Ten employees work as a group. The standard output for the group is 200 units per hour and when this is exceeded each employee in the group is paid a bonus in addition to the hourly wage.

The bonus percentage is calculated as follows:

$$50\% \times \frac{\text{Excess units}}{\text{Standard units}}$$

Each employee in the group is then paid as a bonus this percentage of an hourly wage rate of £7.20 no matter what the individual's hourly wage rate is:

The following is one week's record of production by the group:

	Hours worked	Production units
Monday	90	24,500
Tuesday	88	20,600
Wednesday	90	24,200
Thursday	84	20,100
Friday	88	20,400
Saturday	40	10,200
	480	120,000

Solution

The standard number of units for the time worked

$480 \times 200 = 96,000$ units

The number of excess units produced

$120,000 - 96,000 = 24,000$ units

The bonus calculation

$24,000/96,000 \times 50\% = 0.125$

Individual hourly bonus

$£7.20 \times 0.125 = 0.9$

Group bonus

$480 \times 0.9 = £432$

If Jones worked for 42 hours and was paid £6.00 per hour as a basic rate what would be his total pay for this week?

Basic	=	42×6	=	£252
Bonus	=	42×0.9	=	£37.8
Total			=	£289.8

2.8 Holiday pay

As well as the normal payments of wages and salaries, there are other labour costs which include holiday pay and training time.

Holiday pay is non-productive, but it is nevertheless charged to the cost of production by allocating the full year's holiday pay to overhead and charging it to production for the whole year.

Alternatively, wages may be allocated at **labour rates inflated to include holiday pay** and other non-productive time costs.

2.9 Training time and supervisors' wages

Wages paid during a period of **training** may be charged partly to the job and partly to production overhead. The fact that learners work more slowly than trained employees is offset by the learners' lower rate of pay. Apprentices' remuneration will be charged to a separate account.

Normally, **supervisors' wages** are treated as part of department overhead unless only a particular job is concerned. Where instruction is being given, the remuneration of instructors and supervisors may be included in training time.

2.10 Summary

Different types of employee in an organisation will be paid in different ways. For example, management are normally paid by salary, production workers will be either hourly paid or paid on a piecework basis and the sales team may well be paid according to a bonus scheme.

3 Direct and indirect labour costs

3.1 Recap on direct and indirect costs

- A **direct** cost is an item of cost that is traceable directly to a cost unit.

- An **indirect** cost is a cost that either cannot be identified with any one finished unit. Such costs are often referred to as "overheads".

We have seen that there are a variety of different methods of remunerating employees and a number of different elements to this remuneration. For costing purposes the total labour costs must be split between the **direct labour costs**, which can be charged to the units of **production** and any **indirect labour costs**, which are charged as **overheads** to the relevant cost centre.

3.2 Production workers

The wages that are paid to the production workers will **on the whole be direct labour costs** so long as they **relate directly** to the production of output, known as basic rate. The direct labour cost will also include the basic rate for any overtime hours but the **overtime premium** may be treated as an indirect cost.

3.3 Overtime premium

Whether the overtime premium is treated as a direct or indirect labour cost will depend upon the reasons for the overtime:

- If the overtime were worked due to a customer's specific instruction, then the overtime premium will be treated as a direct labour cost.

- If the overtime were due to general pressure of work, then the premium is treated as an indirect labour cost.

3.4 Holiday pay

Holiday pay is normally treated as an **indirect** labour cost as **no production** is occurring.

3.5 Training time

The hours paid for the labour force to train are treated as an **indirect** labour cost as **no production** is occurring.

3.6 Idle time

Controllable idle time is treated as an indirect labour cost. Uncontrollable idle time is treated as an expense in the costing profit and loss account.

It should obviously be prevented as far as possible. It is important to analyse the causes of idle time so that necessary corrective action can be taken. There are three groups of causes of idle time:

(a) Productive causes (e.g. machine breakdown, power failure or time spent waiting for work, tools, materials or instructions).

(b) Administrative causes (e.g. surplus capacity, policy changes, unforeseen drop in demand).

(c) Economic causes (e.g. seasonal fluctuations in demand, cyclical fluctuations in demand, changes in demand because of tax changes).

3.7 Management and supervisor's salaries

Management salaries and supervisor's salaries are all labour costs that are **not related to actual production** of the cost units, therefore they are all treated as **indirect labour costs**.

Activity 6

G Dickson is a football manufacturer . Classify the following costs by nature (direct or indirect) in the table below.

Cost	Direct	Indirect
Basic pay for production workers		
Supervisors wages		
Bonus for salesman		
Production workers overtime premium due to general pressures.		
Holiday pay for production workers		
Sick pay for supervisors		
Time spent by production workers cleaning the machinery		

---

4 Integrated bookkeeping - labour

4.1 Introduction

The costs of a business have to be recorded in a bookkeeping system. Many businesses use an **intergrated bookkeeping system** where the ledger accounts kept provide the necessary **information for both costing and financial accounting**.

4.2 Labour cost account

The labour cost account is where the movement of the costs associated with the labour are recorded.

Example

Labour cost account

	£		£
Bank (1)	80	Production (2)	60
		Production Overheads (3)	20
	___		___
	80		80
	___		___

(1) Labour costs **incurred** are paid out of the **bank** before they are analysed further in the labour account.

(2) The majority of the labour costs incurred by a manufacturing organisation are in respect of **direct labour costs**. Direct labour costs are directly involved in production and are transferred out of the labour account via a credit entry to the production account. The production account can also be referred to as Work in Progress (WIP).

(3) **Indirect labour costs** include indirect labour (costs of indirect labour workers), overtime premium (unless overtime is worked at the specific request of a customer), shift premium, sick pay and idle time. All of these indirect labour costs are collected in the production overheads account. They are transferred there via a credit entry out of the labour account and then debited in the production overheads account

---

Activity 7

What are the correct journal entries the following accounting transactions:

1. Payment for labour:

    A   Dr Bank, Cr Labour

    B   Dr Trade Creditors Control, Cr Labour

    C   Dr Labour, Cr Bank

    D   Dr Labour, Cr Trade Creditors Control

2. Analysis of direct labour:

A   Dr Bank, Cr Labour

B   Dr Labour, Cr Bank

C   Dr Labour, Cr Production

D   Dr Production, Cr Labour

3. Analysis of payment for labour relating to overtime premium that was due to a specific customer request:

A   Dr Production, Cr Labour

B   Dr Production Overheads, Cr Labour

C   Dr Labour, Cr Production

D   Dr Labour, Cr Production Overheads

4. Analysis of payment for labour relating to overtime premium that was due to general work pressures.

A   Dr Labour, Cr Production

B   Dr Labour, Cr Production Overheads

C   Dr Production, Cr Labour

D   Dr Production Overheads, Cr Labour

5 Summary

This chapter has considered the **methods of payment** of labour that may be used by organisations. These may be annual salaries, hourly rates of pay, performance related pay (piecework) and profit related pay (bonus schemes). In order to pay the correct amount to employees there must be detailed recording of the time spent at work by each employee on time sheets or by a time clock and clock cards.

The distribution between **direct and indirect labour** costs is an important one.

Direct labour costs including the following:

- production workers' wages (excluding overtime premiums)

- bonus payments for production workers

- overtime premiums where overtime was worked at the specific request of the customer.

Indirect labour costs include the following:

- holiday pay

- training time

- idle time

- supervisors' salaries

- management salaries

- overtime premiums where overtime was due to the general pressure of work.

- production supervisor's wages that cannot be allocated to specific cost units.

 Test your knowledge

Having completed Chapter 3 you should now be able to attempt:

Practice Activities 13, 14 and 15

Answers to chapter activities

Activity 1

Employee's weekly timesheet for week ending 12 December

Name:	Thomas Yung	Cost centre:	Machining
Employee number: Y4791		Basic Pay per hour: £12	

	Hours spent on:		Notes	Basic pay £	Overtime premium £	Total pay £
	Production	Indirect work				
Monday	6	2	1 - 3pm cleaning machinery	96	12	108
Tuesday	2	4	9am – 1pm training course	72	0	72
Wednesday	8			96	12	108
Thursday	6			72	0	72
Friday	6	1	2-3pm health and safety training	84	6	90
Saturday	6			72	36	108
Sunday	3			0	72	72
Total	37	7		492	138	630

Activity 2

Basic	= 40 × 5	= £200
Overtime	= 5 × 5 × 1.5	= £37.50
Total pay		= £237.50

Answer B

Activity 3

Answer: multiply the quantity by the standard time per item for each item to give a standard time of 39 hours. This is multiplied by the rate per standard hour. 39 × £6.20 = £241.80

Answer C   £241.80

 Activity 4

Total weekly wage:

	£
Monday (12 × £3)	36
Tuesday (14 × £3)	42
Wednesday (guarantee)	28
Thursday (14 × £3)	42
Friday (guarantee)	28
	176

Answer A

 Activity 5

Total weekly wage:

	£
Monday (12 × £3)	36
Tuesday (14 × £3)	42
Wednesday (9 × £3)	27
Thursday (14 × £3)	42
Friday (8 × £3)	24
	171

As the weekly earnings are above £140, the guaranteed amount is not relevant to the calculations in this instance.

Answer D

KAPLAN PUBLISHING

Activity 6

Cost	Direct	Indirect
Basic pay for production workers	☑	
Supervisors wages		☑
Bonus for salesman		☑
Production workers overtime premium due to general pressures.		☑
Holiday pay for production workers		☑
Sick pay for supervisors		☑
Time spent by production workers cleaning the machinery		☑

 Activity 7

1   Payment for labour:

      C Dr Labour, Cr Bank

2   Analysis of direct labour:

      D Dr Production, Cr Labour

3   Analysis of payment for labour relating to overtime premium that was due to a specific customer request:

      A Dr Production, Cr Labour

4   Analysis of payment for labour relating to overtime premium that was due to general work pressures.

      D Dr Production Overheads, Cr Labour

Expenses

4

Introduction

All other costs that are not material or labour related are known as expenses. This chapter looks at the distinction between different types of expense, how expenses are recorded and capital and revenue expenditure.

KNOWLEDGE

Explain the purpose of internal reporting and providing accurate information to management in terms of decision making, planning and control (1.1)

SKILLS

Record and analyse costs in accordance with the organisation's costing procedures (1.1)

Analyse cost information for materials, labour and expenses (1.2)

CONTENTS

1 Expenses
2 Direct and indirect expenses
3 Recording expenses
4 Capital and revenue expenditure

1 Expenses

1.1 Introduction

Costs incurred by a business, other than material and labour costs, are known as expenses.

Expenses of a business can cover a wide variety of areas. They might include:

- rent and rates
- electricity and power costs
- hire of machinery
- royalties
- patent costs
- sub-contractors costs
- insurance
- food for the canteen
- petrol for the delivery vans
- depreciation (depreciation provides a way of spreading the cost of a fixed asset over the life of the asset)

The list could go on and we will consider many of these later in this chapter and in the next chapter.

2 Direct and indirect expenses

2.1 Introduction

Remember that direct costs are those that can be related directly to a **cost unit,** whilst indirect costs (overheads) cannot be specifically traced to individual units.

2.2 Direct expenses

Expenses are far more likely to be indirect; however, some examples of direct expenses are given below.

Note that direct expenses are production costs.

- **Royalty or patent costs** payable for use of a particular component, technique, trade name, etc in the production or service.

- **Sub-contracted charges**: if the business hires another company or a self-employed person to perform a particular function directly related to the product or service provided, this will be treated as a direct expense.

- Expenses associated with **machinery or equipment** used for a particular job: hire charges, maintenance, power, etc.

Note that payments to a sub-contractor are not treated as labour costs but as a direct expense.

For example, a building contractor will very often use sub-contractors to carry out electrical and plumbing work on a particular contract. The charge invoiced to the builder for this work (which will include both labour and materials) will be analysed as a direct expense of the contract.

2.3 Indirect expenses (overheads)

Indirect expenses are far more common and can be categorised in various ways, depending upon the organisational structure of the business and the level of detail required in the cost accounts.

Depending upon their nature, indirect expenses may be:

- production costs (production overheads); or

- non-production costs (non-production overheads).

2.4 Production overheads

We saw earlier that production overheads (although an indirect cost) are included in the total production cost of the product. They will include factory rent, rates, insurance, light, heat, power and other factory running costs; plant and machinery depreciation (see later in the chapter) and production service centres (works canteen, maintenance department, etc).

For a **service business**, it is more difficult to make a clear distinction between production and non-production overheads. For example, there is rarely a building that is devoted entirely to the provision of the service itself (i.e. equivalent to a factory) that does not also house the administrative, financial, selling and other functions of the business. Thus it is common to include most, if not all, of a service business's expenses under the other functional headings described below.

2.5 Non-production overheads

(a) Administrative costs

These are usually: non-productive buildings running costs; staff and other expenses for the accounts, secretarial, data processing, general maintenance and other support service departments; management salaries and motor vehicle expenses; training costs.

(b) Selling and distribution costs

These are usually: sales persons' salaries, commissions, etc; running costs of sales showrooms and offices; delivery vehicle expenses; packaging costs; advertising and promotional costs.

(c) Finance costs

These are usually: loan and overdraft interest payable; bank charges; lease interest element; cost of bad debts.

(d) Legal and professional charges

These are usually: auditors', accountants', solicitors', financial advisors' fees; professional subscriptions; professional indemnity insurance; licence costs.

These headings are, of course, only one possible way to analyse expenses (by function). One of the alternatives could be by **nature** (i.e. staff costs, buildings costs, fixtures, fittings and equipment costs).

It is necessary to be very clear of the distinction between direct/indirect and production/non-production costs when discussing expenses.

Activity 1

RFB plc makes wheels for a variety of uses: wheelbarrows, carts, toys, etc.

Complete the following form by putting a tick for each of the cost items into the appropriate column.

	Prime cost £	Production expense £	Admin expense £	Selling and distribution expense £
Wages of assembly employees				
Wages of stores employees				
Tyres for toy wheels				
Safety goggles for operators				

Job advert for new employees				
Depreciation of salesmen's cars				
Depreciation of production machines				
Cost of trade exhibition				
Computer stationery				
Course fee for AAT training				
Royalty for the design of Wheel 1477				

3 Recording expenses

3.1 Allocation to cost centres

For control purposes, all costs eventually need to be **allocated to cost centres and/or cost units**. For materials and labour costs, this may be achieved by use of coded materials requisitions or analysed timesheets. The same principle will apply to expenses, although the allocation of indirect expenses may be done in stages

The general approach to expense recording and allocation will be as follows.

3.2 Direct expenses

When the invoice arrives (e.g. from a sub-contractor), the relevant product/job/client will be identified and the invoice **coded** accordingly before being passed to the data processing department for recording in the ledgers.

3.3 Indirect expenses

These, by definition, will not be directly identifiable with a particular cost unit and will therefore initially be charged to an **appropriate cost centre**.

Some expenses will relate solely to **one cost centre**.

For example, advertising invoices will be allocated to the marketing/selling department and petrol bills for delivery vehicles will be charged to distribution. The invoices can therefore be coded to the appropriate centre.

Many expenses will, however, relate to **more than one cost centre** – for example, rent, rates and other buildings costs, where the building is shared by several cost centres.

Ultimately, these costs will need to be **shared between the appropriate cost** centres using some agreed basis (e.g. floor area occupied). The topic of such overhead apportionment is covered in detail in the next chapter.

Initially, however, the invoiced expense will generally be coded to a '**collecting**' cost centre for such costs – for example, building costs may be defined as a cost centre in itself. The subsequent apportionment will then be made as a set of transfers from this centre to the appropriate organisational cost centres.

3.4   Documentation

Most expenses will be documented by way of a **supplier's invoice or bill**. The authorisation for payment, codings for posting to the appropriate ledger accounts/cost centres and other internally added information may be attached by way of a standard **ink stamp** with appropriate boxes for manual completion

As with materials and labour, expense invoices will also be coded to indicate whether they are direct expenses or to which cost centre they are to be allocated if they are indirect expenses.

 Capital and revenue expenditure

4.1   Introduction

One particular distinction in expenditure classification is between capital expenditure and revenue expenditure.

4.2 Capital expenditure

 Definition

Capital expenditure is expenditure incurred in:

(a) the acquisition of fixed assets required for use in the business and not for resale

(b) the alteration or improvement of fixed assets for the purpose of increasing their revenue-earning capacity.

4.3 Revenue expenditure

 Definition

Revenue expenditure is expenditure incurred in:

(a) the acquisition of assets acquired for conversion into cash (e.g. goods for resale)

(b) the manufacturing, selling and distribution of goods and the day-to-day administration of the business

(c) the **maintenance** of the revenue-earning capacity of the fixed assets (i.e. repairs, etc).

In practice, there can be some **difficulty** in clearly distinguishing between alteration/improvement of fixed assets (capital) and their maintenance (revenue). For example, is the installation of a modern heating system to replace an old inefficient system an improvement or maintenance? However, you should not need to make such decisions in your assessment.

4.4 The accounting treatments

Capital expenditure is initially shown in the balance sheet as fixed assets. It is then charged to profit and loss over a number of periods, via the depreciation charge.

Revenue expenditure is generally charged to the profit and loss account for the period in which the expenditure was incurred.

Activity 2

RFB plc makes wheels for a variety of uses: wheelbarrows, carts, toys, etc.

Complete the following form by putting a tick for each of the cost items into the appropriate column.

	Capital Expenditure	Revenue Expenditure
Purchase of a lorry		
Electricity and power costs		
Purchase of a chair for the office		
Road tax for the lorry		
Purchase of premises		
Repair of a broken window		

4.5 The relevance of the distinction to cost accounting

Cost accounting is mainly directed towards gathering and analysing cost information to assist management in planning, control and decision-making. In particular:

(a) the determination of **actual and budgeted costs** and profits for a period and for individual cost centres and cost units

(b) the valuation of **stocks** (raw materials, finished goods, etc).

Thus **revenue expenditure** is of far greater relevance than capital expenditure. The main impact of capital expenditure on the above will be the depreciation charges that arise and that may be charged as a direct product/service cost (as in the depreciation of machinery or equipment used in production or provision of a service) or as an overhead (depreciation of buildings, motor vehicles, etc).

5 Summary

We have now seen how expenses cover all expenditure that is not related to materials or labour. It is important that you are able to distinguish between **direct and indirect expenses**. Direct expenses are any expenses that can be related specifically to a cost unit. Indirect expenses are far more common and are known as overheads.

The distinction between **capital and revenue expenditure** is also important. You must be able to decide whether an expense is capital or revenue in nature. Revenue expenditure is written off to the profit and loss account in the period in which it is incurred, whilst capital expenditure is written off to the profit and loss account over a number of accounting periods, via a depreciation charge.

 Test your knowledge

Having completed Chapter 4 you should now be able to attempt:

Practice Activity 16

Answers to chapter activities

Activity 1

	Prime cost £	Production expense £	Admin expense £	Selling and distribution expense £
Wages of assembly employees	☑			
Wages of stores employees		☑		
Tyres for toy wheels	☑			
Safety goggles for operators		☑		
Job advert for new employees			☑	
Depreciation of salesmen's cars				☑
Depreciation of production machines		☑		
Cost of trade exhibition				☑
Computer stationery			☑	
Course fee for AAT training			☑	
Royalty for the design of Wheel 1477	☑			

Activity 2

RFB plc makes wheels for a variety of uses: wheelbarrows, carts, toys, etc.

Complete the following form by putting a tick for each of the cost items into the appropriate column.

	Capital Expenditure	Revenue Expenditure
Purchase of a lorry	☑	
Electricity and power costs		☑
Purchase of a chair for the office		☑
Road tax for the lorry		☑
Purchase of premises	☑	
Repair of a broken window		☑

Absorption and marginal costing 5

Introduction

Absorption and marginal costing are two different ways of valuing the cost of goods sold and finished goods in stock. With **absorption costing fixed overhead** are treated as a **product cost** and an amount is assigned to each unit. In **marginal costing fixed overheads** are treated as **period costs** and are charged in full against the profit for the period. You need to understand the difference between the two methods and what the effect of stock valuation is on reported profits.

KNOWLEDGE

Explain the relationship between the various costing and accounting systems within an organisation (1.2)

Identify costs and the correct classification: fixed, variable, semi-variable and stepped (2.2)

Identify the differences between marginal and absorption costing (2.3)

SKILLS

Record and analyse costs in accordance with the organisation's costing procedures (1.1)

Analyse cost information for materials, labour and expenses (1.2)

CONTENTS

1 Absorption and marginal costing
2 Changing stock levels
3 Advantages of absorption and marginal costing
4 Contribution and profit

1 Absorption and marginal costing

1.1 Absorption costing

Absorption costing values each unit at the cost incurred to produce the unit. This includes the adds an amount to the cost of each unit to represent the fixed production overheads incurred by that product. The amount added to each unit is based on estimates made at the start of the period.

To calculate a fixed cost per unit the budgeted fixed costs are divided by the budgeted activity. The calculation of the fixed cost per unit is looked at in more detail in chapter 6.

The proforma layout for calculating budgeted profit and loss under absorption costing is as follows (with illustrative figures).

	£
Sales (10,000 × £10)	100,000
Cost of sales (at full **production** cost, £9)	(90,000)
Gross profit	10,000
Less: **Non-production** costs	(2,000)
Profit for the period	8,000

1.2 Marginal costing

Marginal costing values units at the amount of variable costs required by each unit (the marginal cost). This includes direct materials, direct labour, direct expenses and variable overheads. No fixed overheads are absorbed into product costs; they are treated as a period cost and deducted in full lower down the profit and loss account.

The proforma layout for calculating budgeted profit and loss under marginal costing is as follows (with illustrative figures).

	£	£
Sales (10,000 × £10)		100,000
Cost of sales (at **marginal/variable** cost, £6)		60,000
Contribution		40,000
Less: **Fixed** production costs	30,000	
Fixed non-production costs	2,000	
		(32,000)
Profit for the period		8,000

1.3 Comparison of absorption and marginal costing

Below is a table that compares absorption costing and marginal costing:

Absorption costing	Marginal costing
Costs are split based on **function** – production or non-production	Costs are split based on **behaviour** – variable or fixed
Sales – production costs = gross profit	Sales – marginal (variable) costs = contribution
Fixed costs are production costs	Fixed cost are period costs
Non-production overheads are excluded from the cost of sales	Fixed non-production overheads are excluded from the cost of sales

Activity 1

The following information has been provided.

	Cost per unit £
Direct material	8.50
Direct labour	27.20
Variable production overhead	11.30
Fixed production overhead	14.00
Selling price	61.50

KAPLAN PUBLISHING

101

Required

Calculate each of the following in £/unit:

(a)   prime cost

(b)   marginal cost

(c)   absorption cost

(d)   gross profit

(e)   contribution

2   Changing stock levels

2.1   Introduction

Another consequence of the difference in stock valuation between marginal and absorption costing is that reported profits may differ if there is closing stock. This is because:

- under **marginal costing** all the period's fixed production overheads are charged **in full** against that period's profit, whereas

- under **absorption costing** some of the period's fixed production overheads will be **carried forward** in the closing stock value and charged to the next period's profit and loss.

The cost of sales calculation in the budgeted profit and loss can be broken down into 3 elements - opening stock, production and closing stock. The units within these elements are valued either at marginal cost or absorption cost. The value of the closing stock is subtracted from the sum of the value of the opening stock and production to calculate the cost of making sales.

This is illustrated in the following example

Example

Worked example of profit differences

	£ per unit
Sales price	£15
Direct materials	£4
Variable production costs	£2

Budgeted fixed production overheads	£40,000 per month
Budgeted production	10,000 units per month
Budgeted sales	8,000 units

No opening stock.

Required

Produce a budgeted marginal costing and an absorption costing profit and loss account for a month

Solution

When calculating the profit we will need the number of units in closing stock. This is given by:

Opening stock + production – sales

This will be 0 + 10,000 – 8,000 = 2,000 units

Marginal costing profit and loss account

	£	£
Sales (8,000 × £15)		120,000
Opening stock	–	
Marginal costs (10,000 × £6)	60,000	
Closing stock (2,000 × £6)	(12,000)	
	———	
Marginal cost of sales		(48,000)
		———
Contribution		72,000
Fixed costs		(40,000)
		———
Profit		32,000
		———

The marginal cost is calculated by adding together all the variable costs. In this example the direct materials and the variable production costs are both variable. The fixed costs are charged in full against the sales for the period.

Absorption costing profit and loss account

	£	£
Sales (8,000 × £15)		120,000
Opening stock	–	
Production costs (10,000 × £10)	100,000	
Closing stock (2,000 × £10)	(20,000)	
	───────	
Cost of sales		(80,000)
		───────
Profit		40,000
		───────

The production cost includes the prime cost of production plus an amount per unit for the fixed production costs.

The fixed overhead absorbed by each unit is as follows.

$$\frac{\text{Budgeted fixed overheads}}{\text{Budgeted production}} = \frac{£40,000}{10,000} = £4 \text{ per unit}$$

Absorption costing reports an £8,000 higher profit than marginal costing. Why?

• Under absorption costing the value of closing stock is £8,000 higher as it includes £4 of fixed costs per unit (2000 units × £4 = £8000).

• Under marginal costing the value of the closing stock is calculated only on the marginal (variable costs). All the fixed costs are charged against the sales as a period charge.

• The closing stock is subtracted from the cost of sales making the cost of sales lower (less cost). In absorption costing we are removing more cost in the closing stock than under marginal costing therefore the profit is higher under absorption costing.

Activity 2

XYZ plc

XYZ plc manufactures toy horses and has produced a budget for the quarter ended 30 June 20X5 (Quarter 1) as follows.

Sales	190 units @ selling price of £12
Production	200 units
Variable production cost per unit	£8
Fixed production costs	£200

There was no opening stock.

Required

Draft the profit statement using:

(i)   marginal costing principles

	£	£
Sales		
Opening Stock		
Marginal costs		
Closing stock	( )	
Cost of sales		( )
Contribution		
Fixed costs		( )
Profit		

(i)   absorption costing principles.

	£	£
Sales		
Opening stock		
Production costs		
Closing stock	( )	
Cost of sales		( )
Gross profit		
Non-production costs		
Profit		

Activity 3

McTack

McTack manufactures PCs and has produced a budget for the quarter ended 31 March 20X4 (Quarter 1) using absorption costing as follows.

	£	£
Sales (100 units @ £500 per unit)		50,000
Production cost of 120 units		
Materials	12,000	
Labour	24,000	
Variable overhead	6,000	
Fixed overhead	6,000	
	48,000	
Less: Closing stock (20 × £400)	(8,000)	
		(40,000)
		10,000

Required

Re-draft the profit statement using marginal costing principles.

	£	£
Sales		
Opening Stock		
Marginal costs		
Closing stock	( )	
Cost of sales		( )
Contribution		
Fixed costs		( )
Profit		

3 Advantages of absorption and marginal costing

3.1 Advantages of absorption costing

1 Meets the requirements for financial reporting.

2 The importance of fixed costs is revealed.

3 Where sales are seasonal and production steady the profit figure, being more consistent with production, will be more reasonable.

4 Used for calculating a selling price for the units.

3.2 Advantages of marginal costing

1 Simplicity – avoiding apportionments and absorption problems (see chapter 6).

2 Fixed costs logically relate to time and so are charged as period costs

3 Profit figures more consistent with fluctuating sales.

4 Used for short term decision-making (see below and chapter 10).

4 Contribution and profit

4.1 Contribution

The concept of contribution is one of the most fundamental in cost accounting. Contribution measures the difference between the sales price of a unit and the variable costs of making and selling that unit. We have seen Contribution in the margin costing profit and loss statement:

Sales (10,000 x £10)	100,000
Cost of sales (at **marginal/variable** cost, £6)	60,000
	———
Contribution	**40,000**
Less: **Fixed** production costs	(30,000)
	———
Profit for the period	10,000
	———

4.2 Changes in activity level

There is a direct link between the total contribution and the number of items sold. If sales doubled to 20,000 units the total contribution would also double to £80,000.

How does contribution and profit change if we double output and sales?

	10,000 units		20,000 units
	£		
Sales 10,000 × £10	100,000	20,000 × £10	200,000
Variable costs 10,000 × £6	60,000	20,000 × £6	120,000
	————		————
Contribution	40,000		80,000
Fixed overheads	30,000		30,000
	————		————
Profit	10,000		50,000
	————		————
Contribution per unit	£4		£4
Profit per unit	£1		£2.50

If sales double then the total contribution doubles but profit increases 5 fold. This shows that there is a direct relationship between the number of sales made and the value of contribution but not level of profit.

What happens to profit if sales increase by one extra unit from 10,000 to 10,001?

	£
Sales 10,001 × £10	100,010
Variable costs 10,001 × £6	60,006
	————
Contribution	40,004
Fixed costs	30,000
	————
Profit	10,004
	————

Total contribution increases £4, but as the total fixed overheads does not change **profit therefore also goes up by £4 (i.e. the same as contribution).**

There is therefore **no direct link between profit and output.** If output doubles, profits do not necessarily double.

The concept of **contribution** is an extremely important one in cost and management accounting. It is important to remember that since contribution measures the **difference between sales price and the variable cost of making a unit**, if a product has a positive contribution it is worth making. Any amount of contribution, however small, **goes towards paying the fixed overheads**; if enough units are made and sold such that total contribution exceeds fixed overheads then profit will start to be made.

5 Summary

Marginal costing calculates the **contribution** per unit of a product. In marginal costing units are valued at **variable production cost** and fixed overheads are accounted for as period costs.

In **absorption costing**, units are valued at **variable cost plus fixed production overheads** absorbed using a pre-determined absorption rate.

The differences in these methods give rise to different profit figures which are usually reconciled at the end of an accounting period.

Test your knowledge

Having completed Chapter 5 you should now be able to attempt:

Practice Activities 17 and 18

Answers to chapter activities

Activity 1

(a) Prime cost per unit

	£
Direct material	8.50
Direct labour	27.20
	35.70

(b) Marginal cost per unit

	£
Prime cost	35.70
Variable production overhead	11.30
	47.00

(c) Absorption cost per unit

	£
Prime cost	35.70
Variable production overhead	11.30
Fixed production overhead	14.00
	61.00

(d) Gross profit per unit

	£
Selling price	61.50
Less: Absorption cost	(61.00)
	0.50

(e) Contribution per unit

Selling price	61.50
Less: Marginal cost per unit	47.00
	14.50

KAPLAN PUBLISHING

Activity 2

There will be closing stock of 200 – 190 = 10 units.

Under marginal costing, the closing stock will be valued at the variable production cost of £8 per unit.

With absorption costing the fixed production costs will also have to be included. The £200 fixed production costs will be absorbed into the 200 units of production, giving a fixed cost per unit of £1 and a total absorption cost of 8 + 1 = £9 per unit.

Marginal costing profit and loss account

	£	£
Sales (190 × £12)		2,280
Opening Stock	0	
Marginal costs (200 × £8)	1,600	
Closing stock (10 × £8)	(80)	
Cost of sales		(1,520)
Contribution		760
Fixed costs		(200)
Profit		560

Absorption costing profit and loss account

	£	£
Sales (190 × £12)		2,280
Opening Stock	0	
Production costs (200 × £9)	1,800	
Closing stock (10 × £9)	(90)	
Cost of sales		(1,710)
Gross profit		570
Non-production costs		(0)
Profit		570

Activity 3

McTack – Budgeted profit statement quarter ended 31 March

Marginal costing format

Marginal costing profit and loss account

	£	£
Sales (100 × £500)		50,000
Opening Stock	0	
Marginal costs (12,000 + 24,000 + 6,000)	42,000	
Closing stock (20 × £350)	(7,000)	
Cost of sales		(35,000)
Contribution		15,000
Fixed costs		(6,000)
Profit		9,000

Calculation of marginal cost per unit.

Marginal cost/number of units produced = marginal cost per unit

42,000/120 = £350

Reconciliation of profits	£
Marginal costing	9,000
Add: Fixed overheads in absorption closing stock (20 × £50)	1,000
Absorption costing profit	10,000

Accounting for overheads

Introduction

This chapter looks at how **overheads** (indirect expenses) are **allocated** or **apportioned** to cost centres and how overheads are then **absorbed** into the cost of a product via an **overhead absorption rate**. This chapter applies **absorption costing princples.**

KNOWLEDGE

Identify the bases of allocation and apportioning indirect costs to responsibility centres: direct and step down methods (2.4)

Identify the bases of absorption, and the reasons for their use: machine hours and labour hours (2.5)

SKILLS

Attribute overhead costs to production and service cost centres in accordance with agreed bases of allocation and apportionment (2.1)

Calculate overhead absorption rates in accordance with agreed bases of absorption (2.2)

Make adjustments for under and over recovered costs in accordance with established procedures (2.3)

Review methods of allocation, apportionment and absorption at regular intervals and implement agreed changes to methods (2.4)

Communicate with relevant staff to resolve any queries in overhead cost data (2.5)

CONTENTS

1 Allocation and apportionment of overhead
2 Primary apportionment
3 Secondary apportionment
4 Absorption of overheads
5 Under/over absorption of overheads
6 Integrated bookkeeping - overheads
7 Non-production overheads

1 Allocation and apportionment of overheads

1.1 Indirect costs or overheads

We have seen in earlier chapters of this text that there are three categories of indirect costs (making up total overheads):

- indirect materials
- indirect labour costs
- indirect expenses

There are also two types of indirect costs or overheads:

- **production** overheads (**included** in cost per unit)
- **non-production** overheads (**not included** in cost per unit)

This inclusion of the indirect production costs, or overheads, in the total cost of the cost units is achieved by a process of **allocation** of overheads, **apportionment** of overheads and the **absorption** of overheads.

1.2 Overview of the process of allocation, apportionment and absorption

The purpose of allocation and apportionment is to attribute all production overhead costs to a production cost centre (remember we are not dealing with non- production overheads here). The purpose of absorption is to include the production overheads of a cost centre in the costs of the units produced by the cost centre.

Where a business has a mix of production and service cost centres, it may be necessary to allocate and apportion costs to both types of centre and then reapportion the service centres' costs to the production centres.

There are 3 steps to achieving the process:

Step 1: Overheads are allocated or apportioned to cost centres using suitable bases

Step 2: Any service centre costs are reapportioned to production centres using suitable bases

Step 3: Overheads are absorbed into units of production again using suitable bases

Step 1: Allocation or Apportionm

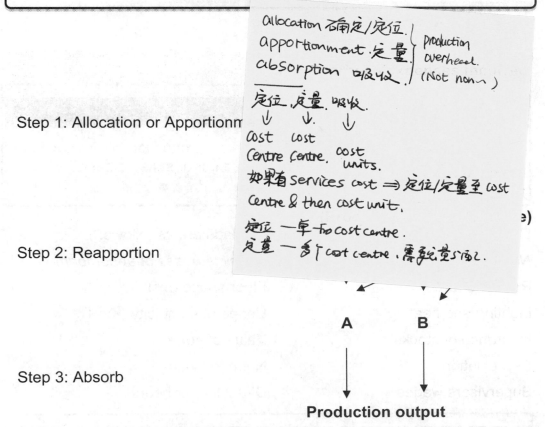

Step 2: Reapportion

A   B

Step 3: Absorb

Production output

Each stage of this process is detailed below.

2 Allocation and apportionment

2.1 Allocation

 Definition

When an overhead relates entirely to one production or service centre it can be wholly attributed to that single production or service centre. This is allocation.

Examples of costs that relate to one specific cost centre are given below:

Cost centre	*Allocated cost*
Accounts	Accounting overhead
Machining department	Insurance of machines
Stores	Stores wages
Canteen	Maintenance of kitchen equipment
Packing department	Depreciation of fork lift trucks

2.2 Apportionment

 Definition

When an overhead relates to more than one production and/or service centre it is shared over these centres on a fair or suitable basis. This is apportionment.

Examples of bases of apportioning overheads are as follows:

Nature of cost	*Possible bases of apportionment*
Rent and rates	Floor space (m^2)
Lighting and heating	Usage of electricity (KwH)
Insurance of stocks	Value of stock
Depreciation	Net book value
Supervisors wages	Direct labour hours

 Example

Example of cost allocation and apportionment

A Ltd has three departments: assembly, machining and administration. It incurs the following indirect costs in the year to December 20X4:

	£
Oil for machining department	2,000
Salary of assembly department supervisor	20,000
Insurance of machines in machining department	4,000
Rent of whole factory and offices	16,000
Administrative salaries	40,000
Canteen costs for whole factory and offices	15,000
	97,000

You are required to:

(a) Allocate the costs that can be allocated to the relevant department.

(b) Apportion the costs that cannot be allocated using the information below:

Department	Assembly	Machining	Administration
Area (sq ft)	3,000	3,000	2,000
No of employees	15	10	5

Solution

Looking at the indirect costs it is possible to identify 4 costs that are wholly attributable to one centre – Oil for **machining**, supervisors' salary for **assembly,** insurance for the machines in the **machining** department and salaries for the administration department. These costs are allocated to specific centres.

The remaining costs relate to more than one centre so need to shared or apportioned across the centre they relate to.

To do this the calculation used is:

$$\frac{\text{Total overhead}}{\text{Total of basis}} \times \text{centre basis}$$

Rent

Assembly

$$\frac{16,000}{8,000} \times 3,000 = 6,000$$

Machining

$$\frac{16,000}{8,000} \times 3,000 = 6,000$$

Administration

$$\frac{16,000}{8,000} \times 2,000 = 4,000$$

Canteen costs

Assembly

$$\frac{15,000}{30} \times 15 = 7,500$$

Machining

$$\frac{15,000}{30} \times 10 = 5,000$$

Administration

$$\frac{15,000}{30} \times 5 = 2,500$$

Overhead cost	Basis of allocation/ apportionment	Total £	Assembly £	Machining £	Administration £
Oil	Allocate	2,000		2,000	
Salary (supervisor)	Allocate	20,000	20,000		
Insurance	Allocate	4,000		4,000	
Rent	Floor area	16,000	6,000	6,000	4,000
Salaries (admin)	Allocate	40,000			40,000
Canteen	No of employees	15,000	7,500	5,000	2,500
		97,000	33,500	17,000	46,500

Activity 1

An organisation has four departments Fixing, Mending, Stores and Canteen.

The overhead costs for the organisation in total are as follows:

	£
Rent	32,000
Building maintenance costs	5,000
Machinery insurance	2,400
Machinery depreciation	11,000
Machinery running expenses	6,000
Power	7,000

There are specific costs that have been allocated to each cost centre as follows:

	£
Fixing	5,000
Mending	4,000
Stores	1,000
Canteen	2,000

The following information about the various cost centres is also available:

	Total	Fixing	Mending	Stores	Canteen
Floor space (sq ft)	30,000	15,000	8,000	5,000	2,000
Power usage	100%	45%	40%	5%	10%
Value of machinery (£000)	250	140	110	–	–
Machinery hours (000)	80	50	30		
Value of equipment (£000)	20	–	–	5	15
Number of employees	40	20	15	3	2
Value of stores requisitions (£000)	150	100	50	–	–

Task

Allocate and apportion the costs to the four departments.

Overhead cost	Basis	Total £	Fixing £	Mending £	Stores £	Canteen £
Specific overheads		12,000				
Rent		32,000				
Building maintenance		5,000				
Machinery insurance		2,400				
Machinery depreciation		11,000				
Machinery running cost		6,000				
Power		7,000				
		75,400				

3 Reapportionment

3.1 Introduction

The next stage in the process is to apportion the service cost centre total costs to the production cost centres that make use of the service cost centre. This process is known as reapportionment or secondary apportionment.

The reason for doing this is that we want all the costs to be identified with a **production** cost centre so that we can then work out the **cost of the** units that the **production** cost centre produces.

3.2 A single service centre

 Example

A business has one service centre, the canteen, that serves two production centres. The overhead costs for a period have been allocated and apportioned between the three departments as given below.

	Production A	Production B	Canteen
Overhead	£10,000	£15,000	£12,000
Number of employees	100	200	

Reapportion the canteen's overheads to the production departments on the basis of the number of employees.

Solution

Exactly the same technique is used to reapportion as is used to apportion.

	Department A £	Department B £	Canteen £
Overhead	10,000	15,000	12,000
Number of employees 1:2	4,000	8,000	(12,000)
Total overhead for production department	14,000	23,000	

Activity 2

The cost of both the stores and the personnel departments of RFB plc have to be apportioned across the other cost centres. What bases would you recommend?

Stores department

A Number of employees

B Floor space

C Number of issues to production

D Kilowatt Hours

Personnel department

A   Number of employees

B   Floor space

C   Number of issues to production

D   Kilowatt Hours

3.3   Two service centres

Problems may arise when there are two or more service centres with costs that have to be identified with production cost centres. There are two situations that need to be considered for this unit:

(a)   The service centres only supply services to the production cost centres ie, they do not provide services to each other.

Production 1   Production 2   Service 1   Service 2

(b)   One of the service centres (number 2 in diagram) provides services to the production cost centres and to the other service centre. The remaining service centre (number 1 in the diagram) only provides services to the production cost centres.

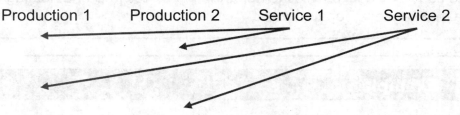

Production 1   Production 2   Service 1   Service 2

3.4   The direct method

This is used in situation (a) above ie, where the service centres do not supply services to each other.

You will typically be given the information about which centre provides services to whom as follows.

Example

A business has two production centres, departments A and B, and two service centres, a canteen and a maintenance department. The proportion of the service departments services supplied to each department is as follows.

	Production A	Production B
Usage of maintenance dept	40%	60%
Usage of canteen	45%	55%

This tells you that the maintenance department supplies 40% of its services to department A, 60% to department B and nothing to the canteen.

The canteen supplies 45% to department A, 55% to B and nothing to the maintenance department.

 Example

If we now add some numbers to the above percentage usage, the calculations will become clear.

The costs allocated and apportioned to the four departments are as follows before any of the service department costs have been apportioned to the production departments.

	£
Production A	50,000
Production B	60,000
Canteen	8,000
Maintenance	10,000

Apportion the service departments costs to the production departments.

Solution

	Dept A £	Dept B £	Canteen £	Maintenance £
	50,000	60,000	8,000	10,000
Reapportionment of maintenance	(40%) 4,000	(60%) 6,000		(10,000)
Reapportionment of canteen	(45%) 3,600	(55%) 4,400	(8,000)	

3.5 The step down method

This is used in situation (b) above ie, where one of the service centres supplies services to the other.

 Example

We shall modify the above example so that the proportion of the service departments services supplied to each department is as follows.

	Production A	Production B	Canteen
Usage of maintenance dept	40%	45%	15%
Usage of canteen	45%	55%	

This tells you that the maintenance department supplies 40% of its services to department A, 45% to department B and 15% to the canteen.

The canteen supplies 45% to department A, 55% to B and nothing to the maintenance department.

Apportion the service departments costs to the production departments.

Solution

	Dept A £	Dept B £	Canteen £	Maintenance £
	50,000	60,000	8,000	10,000
Secondary apportionment of maintenance	(40%) 4,000	(45%) 4,500	(15%) 1,500	(10,000)
Secondary apportionment of canteen	(45%) 4,275	(55%) 5,225	(9,500)	

The method is as follows.

Step 1 Identify the service department whose services are used by the other service department and apportion its costs to all the departments. In this case the maintenance department services the canteen so the maintenance costs are apportioned first.

Step 2 Now apportion the new total costs of the canteen (ie its original costs (£8,000) plus its share of the maintenance costs (£1,500)) to the production departments.

This is referred to as the step down method.

Activity 3

Adam has a factory with two production departments, machining and painting, which are serviced by the maintenance and quality control departments.

Relevant information for a particular period is as follows:

	Machining	Painting	Maintenance	QC
Apportioned overheads (primary)	£20,000	£40,000	£10,000	£15,000
Maintenance	30%	60%		10%
QC	50%	50%		

Task

Show the reapportionment necessary using the step down method and the resulting total overheads to be attributed to each production department.

	Machining		Painting		Maintenance	Quality control	
	£	%	£	%	£	£	%
Apportioned overheads (primary)	20,000		40,000		10,000	15,000	
Reapportionment of maintenance							
Reapportionment of quality control							

 4 **Absorption**

4.1 Introduction

Having collected all indirect costs in the production cost centres via overhead allocation and apportionment/reapportionment, the total overhead of each production cost centre must be charged to the **output of the production cost centres.**

Definition

Overhead absorption is the charging of a production cost centre's overhead costs to the cost units produced by the cost centre.

The **absorption rate** is calculated at the start of the period and is therefore **based on budgeted activity** and on **budgeted overheads**. Various bases of absorption exist and the most suitable one should be chosen depending on the situation.

4.2   One product business

It is possible to calculate the OAR using the planned production in units if only one type of product is being produced. If this is the situation the procedure to assign the correct amount of overhead to each unit is to allocate and apportion the overheads and then calculate how much overhead should be absorbed by each product using the following calculation:

$$\frac{\text{Budgeted Overhead}}{\text{Budgeted Units produced}}$$

Once we know how much overhead each unit is absorbing we can calculate the full production cost per unit.

Example

Henry produces one product. Each unit of the product uses £20 worth of material and £10 of labour. Henry has two production centres, assembly and finishing. The following overheads are expected to be incurred:

Rent and rates   £12,000

Light and heat   £15,000

The assembly department occupies twice the floor area of the finishing department. Production is budgeted for 1,000 units.

Calculate the assembly overhead cost per unit, the finishing overhead cost per unit and hence the total cost per unit.

Solution

Step 1

Apportion the overheads to the cost centres, on the basis of size, therefore in the ratio of 2 to 1.

Overhead	Basis	Total £	Assembly £	Finishing £
Rent and rates	Area 2:1	12,000	8,000	4,000
Light and heat	Area 2:1	15,000	10,000	5,000
		27,000	18,000	9,000

Step 2

Calculate an overhead absorption rate per unit for each department.

Overhead per unit

Assembly

$$\frac{\text{Budgeted Overhead}}{\text{Budgeted Units produced}} = \frac{£18,000}{1,000} = £18 \text{ per unit}$$

Finishing

$$\frac{\text{Budgeted Overhead}}{\text{Budgeted Units produced}} = \frac{£9,000}{1,000} = £9 \text{ per unit}$$

Step 3

	£
Total production cost per unit:	
Direct costs	
Materials	20
Labour	10
Overheads	
Assembly	18
Finishing	9
	57

4.2 Multi-product business

The use of an absorption rate per unit is fine for one-product businesses/cost centres, but **may be inappropriate for multi-product businesses.**

Example

Sam produces pocket calculators and has one production department, having £15,000 overheads. Sam has planned production of 5,000 units.

Overhead absorption rate per unit = $\dfrac{£15,000}{5,000}$ = £3/unit

Suppose Sam instead makes 3,000 pocket calculators and 2,000 complex computers. The complex computers take up twice as much time to produce as the calculators. The total overhead is the same as before. The overhead absorption rate per unit produced will be the same as before:

Overhead absorption rate per unit = $\dfrac{£15,000}{3000 + 2,000}$ = $\dfrac{£15,000}{5,000}$ = £3/unit

Decide whether this is a reasonable basis to absorb overheads.

Solution

This is probably not a reasonable basis. The computer is likely to take longer to make and would involve the use of more of the indirect costs (e.g. supervisor's time). It is therefore necessary to choose an absorption basis that best reflects the demand of that product on the production department through which it passes.

Bases commonly used as an **alternative to the rate per unit**, when more than one product is involved, are as follows.

(a) rate per direct labour hour

(b) rate per machine hour.

The calculaton is as before but rather than dividing by budgeted units it is budgeted activity:

$$\frac{\text{Budgeted Overhead}}{\text{Budgeted Activity}}$$

Whichever method or combination of methods is used, the result will still only be an **approximate estimate** of what each product costs.

Example

Sam makes 3,000 pocket calculators and 2,000 complex computers. The complex computers take up 2 hours to produce and the calculators take only 1 hour to produce. The total overhead is the same as before. The overhead absorption rate per hour produced will be:

$$\text{Overhead absorption rate per unit} = \frac{£15,000}{3000hr + 4,000hr} = \frac{£15,000}{7,000}$$
$$= £2.14/hour$$

This then needs to be assigned on a per unit basis.

The pocket calculators take one hour to produce so will be charged with one hours worth of overhead = £2.14
The complex computers take two hours to produce so will be charged with two hours worth of overhead = £2.14 x 2 = £4.18
The difference in unit overhead charges should reflect the effort that has been made in producing the units.

 Activity 4

Bertram manufactures three products, the cost of each being:

	Apple	Banana	Carrot
Direct materials	£14.40	£25.60	£36.00
Direct labour			
Machining @ £4.80 per hour	2 hours	1.5 hours	2 hours
Assembling @ £3.20 per hour	2 hours	2.5 hours	1 hour

Planned production is:
Product A   10,000 units
Product B   20,000 units
Product C   40,000 units

Production overheads for the forthcoming year are estimated at £120,000.

What would be the budgeted overhead absorption rate per product using the direct labour hour rate?

	Apple £/hr	Banana £/hr	Carrot £/hr
A	1	0.75	1
B	2	2	1.5
C	1	1.25	0.5
D	4	4	3

4.3 Choosing an absorption rate

The choice of which rate to be used depends largely on the nature of the operations concerned.

There is no correct method but in order to produce useful information it will always be preferable to choose an absorption rate which is in some way related to the costs being incurred.

Thus, for example, if the overhead consisted mainly of depreciation of machinery then it would be sensible to use the machine hour rate.
On the other hand, if the overhead consisted mainly of the salaries of supervisors who supervise the workforce then it would make sense to use the labour hour rate.

Example

A factory has two production departments, cutting and finishing. The budgeted overheads and production details are:

	Cutting	Finishing
Budgeted overhead	£100,000	£80,000
Budgeted direct labour hours	10,000	40,000
Budgeted machine hours	60,000	5,000

The cutting department is a machine intensive department whilst finishing is labour intensive.

The factory makes two products, the Pig and the Cow. The production details for these are:

	Pig	Cow
Direct labour hours		
Cutting	1	2
Finishing	4	6
Machine hours		
Cutting	8	6
Finishing	2	2

Calculate the overhead cost to be absorbed into each product using an appropriate absorption rate for each cost centre.

Solution

Step 1 Choose and calculate the absorption rates

It makes sense to use the machine hour rate for the machine intensive cutting department and the labour hour rate for the labour intensive finishing department.

Cutting – machine hour rate $=$ $\dfrac{£100,000}{60,000}$

$=$ £1.67 per machine hour

Finishing – labour hour rate $=$ $\dfrac{£80,000}{40,000}$

$=$ £2 per direct labour hour

Step 2 Absorption into unit costs

		£
Product Pig		
Cutting 8 hours × £1.67		13.36
Finishing 4 hours × £2		8.00
		21.36
Product Cow		
Cutting 6 hours × £1.67		10.02
Finishing 6 hours × £2		12.00
		22.02

As the cutting cost centre is machine intensive then a machine hour absorption rate will best reflect how the overhead is incurred and, as the finishing cost centre is labour intensive, a direct labour hour rate is most appropriate in this cost centre.

Which rate should be used? Possibly both – **it depends upon the nature of the overheads**.

Activity 5

Pears plc manufactures children's clothing. The General Manager (GM) is concerned about how the costs of the various garments it produces are calculated. The material cost varies from one garment to another and the rates of pay in the various departments also vary to reflect the different skills offered. Both these prime costs are charged direct to individual garments so that any variation is taken into account.

	Overhead cost £000	Numbers employed	Labour hours	Material issued £000	Machine hours
Production departments					
Cutting	187	10	400	200	15,000
Sewing	232	15	300	250	25,000
Finishing	106	8	12,000	100	
Service departments					
Stores	28	2		–	
Maintenance	50	3		50	

Using the overhead analysis sheet below, apportion:

(a) (i) stores department's costs to the production and maintenance departments

  (ii) maintenance department's costs to the cutting and sewing departments only.

Select the most suitable basis for each apportionment and state the bases used on the overhead analysis sheet. (Calculations to the nearest £000.)

Overhead analysis sheet

	TOTAL	PRODUCTION			SERVICE	
		Cutting	Sewing	Finishing	Stores	Maintenance
	£000	£000	£000	£000	£000	£000
Overheads	603	187	232	106	28	50
Apportion store Basis:						
Apportion maintenance Basis:						
Total						

(b) What would be the overhead rate for the three production
departments if cutting and sewing where highly mechanised and
finishing required high human input:

	Cutting	Sewing	Finishing
A	14.33	11.08	9.25
B	537.50	923.33	9.25
C	215.00	18.46	13.88
D	14.33	11.08	13.88

5   Under/over absorption of overheads

5.1   Introduction

The **overhead absorption rates** that were calculated in the previous
section are calculated at the start of the accounting period. Therefore they
are based upon **budgeted figures**. This means that the calculation is
based upon the budgeted overhead cost and the budgeted production
details, be it units, labour hours, machine hours, etc.

The reason for this is that management will need to know the **budgeted
cost of each unit of production** in order to be able to make decisions
about the products and the sales and production. This requires not only
budgeted figures for direct materials, direct labour and direct expenses,
but also for overheads.

5.2   Absorption of overheads

During the accounting period the cost of each unit of that is produced will
include overheads based upon the budgeted overhead absorption rate.

But what happens if:

(a) the **actual production levels** are different from the budgeted levels
and/or

(b) the **actual overheads** for the period are different from the budgeted
overheads?

If either or both of these occur, the use of the predetermined absorption
rate will result in an **over- or under-absorption of overheads**.
(Sometimes referred to as over or under recovery of overheads)

Example

A factory budgets to produce 10,000 units, its budgeted overhead is £30,000 and the budgeted direct labour hours are 4,000.

The factory actually produced only a total of 8,000 units in the coming year, due to a machine breakdown, in 3,200 labour hours. In addition, the cost of machine repairs resulted in actual factory overheads amounting to £34,000.

The factory absorbs the overhead based on labour hours.

What is the under- or over-absorbed overhead?

Solution

The over-/under-absorbed overheads can be determined by the comparison of the actual total overhead cost with the overheads that are absorbed during production at the budgeted overhead absorption rate. There is a 3 step calculation to calculate the under- or over-absorption.

Step 1 – calculate the budgeted overhead absorption rate

$$\text{OAR} = \frac{\text{Budgeted Overhead cost}}{\text{Budgeted Activity}}$$

$$= \frac{£30,000}{4,000}$$

$$= £7.50 \text{ per direct labour hour}$$

Step 2 – calculate the overhead absorbed by actual production

Absorbed = OAR × Actual activity
= £7.50 × 3,200 hours

= £24,000

Step 3 – calculate the under- or over-absorption

Under- or
over-absorption = Actual overhead cost – Absorbed overhead cost
= £34,000 - £24,000
= £10,000

The absorbed overhead is less than the actual overhead so there has been an under-absorption of the overhead

Activity 6

The actual overheads for a department were £6,500 last period and the actual output was 540 machine hours. The budgeted overheads were £5,995 and the budgeted output was 550 machine hours.

What is the OAR?
A £11.82
B £10.90
C £12.04
D £11.10

How much overhead will be absorbed into production?
A £6,622
B £5,994
C £5,886
D £6,383

What is the under- or over-absorption of the overheads?
A £122 over
B £506 under
C £614 under
D £117 under

 6 Integrated bookkeeping - overheads

6.1 Introduction

The costs of a business have to be recorded in a bookkeeping system. Many businesses use an **integrated bookkeeping system** where the ledger accounts kept provide the necessary **information for both costing and financial accounting**.

6.2 Production overheads account

The production overhead account is where the movement of the costs associated with the overheads (indirect costs) are recorded.

:'Ö': **Example**

Production Overheads

	£		£
Actual Overhead cost (1)		Absorbed overheads (2)	
Over-absorbed (3)		Under-absorbed (4)	

(1) The **actual cost** of all the indirect costs are recorded as a **debit** in the production overheads account. The credit is either in the bank or creditors acccount. The actual cost will be made up off all the indirect production costs – material, labour and expenses.

(2) The overheads that are **absorbed into production** (WIP) are recorded as a **credit** in the production overhead account. This is calculated as the **budgeted OAR × actual activity**

(3) When the account is balanced at the end of the period and the **balancing amount** is required to make the **debit** side of the account match the credit side we have an **over-absorption** of overheads. The overheads absorbed into production are greater than the actual cost of the overheads.

(4) When the account is balanced at the end of the period and the **balancing amount** is required to make the **credit** side of the account match the debit side we have an **under-absorption** of overheads. The overheads absorbed into production are less than the actual cost of the overheads.

6.3 The adjustment for under-/over-absorption

The adjustment for an **under-absorbed overhead** is made as a **debit** to the costing **profit and loss account**. If the overheads have been under-absorbed we need to **decrease profit** and increase the expense in the costing profit and loss account.

	£
Sales	X
Cost of sales (using budgeted overhead absorption rates)	X
	___
Gross profit	X
Less: Under-absorption of fixed overheads	(10,000)
	___
Adjusted gross profit	X
	___

The accounting entry for this adjustment would be as follows.

		£	£
Debit:	Profit and loss account	10,000	
Credit:	Production overheads		10,000

The adjustment for an **over-absorbed overhead** is made as a **credit** to the costing **profit and loss account**. If the overheads have been over-absorbed we need to **increase profit** and decrease the expense in the costing profit and loss account.

	£
Sales	X
Cost of sales (using budgeted overhead absorption rates)	X
	___
Gross profit	X
Add: Over-absorption of fixed overheads	10,000
	___
Adjusted gross profit	X
	___

The accounting entry for this adjustment would be as follows.

		£	£
Debit:	Production overheads	10,000	
Credit:	Profit and loss account		10,000

Activity 7

What are the correct journal entries the following accounting transactions:

1. Indirect material issued from stores:

   A   Dr Bank, Cr Material

   B   Dr Production Overheads, Cr Material

   C   Dr Material, Cr Bank

   D   Dr Material, Cr Production Overheads

2. Indirect wages analysed in the labour account:

   A   Dr Production, Cr Labour

   B   Dr Labour, Cr Production

   C   Dr Labour, Cr Production Overheads

   D   Dr Production Overheads, Cr Labour

3. Production overheads absorbed into the cost of production:

   A   Dr Production, Cr Production Overheads

   B   Dr Production Overheads, Cr Profit and Loss

   C   Dr Producton Overheads, Cr Production

   D   Dr Profit and Loss, Cr Production Overheads

4. Over-absorption of overheads

   A   Dr Production, Cr Production Overheads

   B   Dr Production Overheads, Cr Profit and Loss

   C   Dr Producton Overheads, Cr Production

   D   Dr Profit and Loss, Cr Production Overheads

7 Non-production overheads

7.1 Introduction

So far, only production overheads have been considered. There are other, non-production overheads which can be divided into the broad categories listed below, all of which can be absorbed into each cost unit using similar methods as described, if desired.

But remember, if the **non-production overheads are absorbed into units**, the **cost per unit will not be the stock value per unit**. The stock value per unit comprises only the production costs, direct and indirect.

7.2 Administrative overheads

Expenditure attributable to the general office, data processing, finance charges and audit fees.

7.3 Selling overheads

Expenditure attributable to the selling of the product, eg sales personnel, costs of advertising, cash discounts allowed, rent and rates of show rooms and sales offices.

7.4 Distribution overheads

Expenditure incurred in packing and delivery.

8 Summary

This chapter has considered how the overheads of a business are gathered together and traced through to the cost units to which they relate. Under the **absorption costing** approach the budgeted overheads of the business are collected together in each of the cost centres, either by **allocation**, if the overhead relates to only one cost centre or by **apportionment** on a fair basis if the overhead relates to a number of cost centres.

Once the overheads have been allocated and apportioned, the next stage is to **reapportion** any **service** cost centre overheads into the production cost centres. Care must be taken here where the service cost centres provide their service to other service cost centres. In these cases the step down method is required to reapportion the service cost centre overheads.

When all of the budgeted overheads are included in the production cost centres, an **absorption rate** must be calculated. In many cases this will be either on a direct labour hour basis or on a machine hour basis. This will depend on the nature of the business and the nature of the cost centre.

The overhead absorption rate is based upon the budgeted overheads and the budgeted production level. This rate is then used to include the overheads in the production throughout the accounting period. If the activity levels and/or the amount of the overhead are different to the budgeted figures, then the overhead will be either **over- or under-absorbed**. An adjustment is made for this when the costing profit and loss account is prepared.

 Test your knowledge

Having completed Chapter 6 you should now be able to attempt:

Practice Activities 19, 20, 21, 22 and 23

Answers to chapter activities

 Activity 1

OVERHEAD ANALYSIS SHEET		PERIOD ENDING			
	Total	Production		Service	
	£	Fixing £	Mending £	Stores £	Canteen £
Overheads allocated directly to cost centres	12,000	5,000	4,000	1,000	2,000
Overheads to be apportioned Rent Basis: floor space 32/30 x 15,000 32/30 x 8,000 32/30 x 5,000 32/30 x 2,000	32,000	16,000	8,534	5,333	2,133
Building maintenance Basis: floor space 5/30 × 15,000 5/30 × 8,000 5/30 × 5,000 5/30 × 2,000	5,000	2,500	1,333	834	333
Machinery insurance Basis: machine value 2400/250 × 140 2400/250 × 110	2,400	1,344	1,056	–	–
Machinery depreciation Basis: machine value 11,000/250 × 140 11,000/250 × 110	11,000	6,160	4,840	–	–
Machinery running expenses Basis: machine hours 6,000/80 × 50 6,000/80 × 30	6,000	3,750	2,250	–	–

	Total	Production		Service	
	£	Fixng £	Mending £	Stores £	Canteen £
Power Basis: power usage percentages £7,000 × 45% £7,000 × 40% £7,000 × 5% £7,000 × 10%	7,000	3,150	2,800	350	700
Allocated and apportioned costs	75,400	37,904	24,813	7,517	5,166

 Activity 2

Stores – C

Personnel – A

 Activity 3

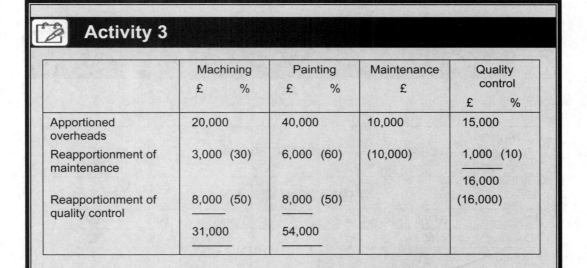

	Machining £ %	Painting £ %	Maintenance £	Quality control £ %
Apportioned overheads	20,000	40,000	10,000	15,000
Reapportionment of maintenance	3,000 (30)	6,000 (60)	(10,000)	1,000 (10)
				16,000
Reapportionment of quality control	8,000 (50)	8,000 (50)		(16,000)
	31,000	54,000		

Activity 4

Answer B

	Apple	Banana	Carrot	Total
Production (units)	10,000	20,000	40,000	70,000
Production hours				
Machining	20,000	30,000	80,000	130,000
Assembly	20,000	50,000	40,000	110,000
Total hours	40,000	80,000	120,000	**240,000**

Fixed overhead per direct labour hour: $\dfrac{£120,000}{240,000} = £0.50$

	Apple £	Banana £	Carrot £
Overheads	(4 hr × £0.50) = 2.00/hr	(4 hr × £0.50) = 2.00/hr	(3 hr × £0.50) = 1.50/hr

Activity 5

(a)

Overhead analysis sheet	TOTAL	PRODUCTION			SERVICE	
		Cutting	Sewing	Finishing	Stores	Maint'nce
	£000	£000	£000	£000	£000	£000
Overheads	603	187	232	106	28	50
Apportion store Basis:		9	12	5	(28)	2
Apportion maint'nce Basis:		19	33			(52)
Total	603	215	277	111		

KAPLAN PUBLISHING

(b)   Answer A

	Cutting	Sewing	Finishing
Apportioned o/heads	£215,000	£277,000	£111,000
Machine hours	15,000	25,000	
Labour hours			12,000
Absorption rates	£14.33	£11.08	£9.25

 Activity 6

(a)   Answer B

£5995/550 hours = £10.90

(b)   Answer C

£10.90 × 540 = £5886

(c)   Answer C

£6500 - £5886 = £614 under-absorbed

 Activity 7

1   Answer B

2   Answer D

3   Answer A

4   Answer B

Job and batch costing systems

7

Introduction

We are now going to turn our attention to two costing systems, job costing and batch costing. **Job costing** involves **individual jobs** with **different materials and labour requirements** (for example, car repairs). **Batch costing,** on the other hand, is suitable for businesses that produce **batches of identical items** (for example, bars of soap) though **batch costs may vary from product to product.**

KNOWLEDGE
Identify the most appropriate costing system: job, batch, unit, process or service (2.6)

SKILLS
Record and analyse costs in accordance with the organisation's costing procedures (1.1)
Analyse cost information for materials, labour and expenses (2.1)

CONTENTS
1 Job costing
2 Batch costing

1 Job costing

1.1 Job costing

Job costing is used in a business where the production is made up of individual large jobs, each of which is different and has different inputs of materials and labour. Each job is identified separately and the costs are identified for this specific job, coded to it and recorded as job costs. Effectively the job is the cost unit.

Typical examples of businesses that use job costing would be construction, aeroplane manufacture, printing and vehicle repairs.

1.2 Job card

Each job is given a separate identifying number and has its own job card. The job card is used to record all of the direct costs of the job and then eventually the overheads to be absorbed into the job.

A typical job card might look like this:

Example

The purchase requisition for 400 litres of oil L04 has been received by the purchasing department.

JOB NO	217		
Materials requisitions	**Quantity**	**£**	**Total**
0254 G 3578	100 kg	4,200	
0261 K 3512	50 kg	3,150	
		——	7,350
Wages – employees	**Hours**	**£**	
13343	80	656	
15651	30	300	
12965	40	360	
	——	——	
	150		1,316
	——		

Overheads	Hours	£	
Absorption rate £12	150	1,800	1,800
			———
Total cost			10,466
			———

1.3 Materials requisitions

When materials are requisitioned then the requisition will be clearly coded to indicate the job to which it relates. The quantity and value of the material will then be recorded on the job card. This happens each time materials are requisitioned for this job.

1.4 Job analysis of gross pay

Where it is required to identify wages or salaries with particular jobs, then in addition to their attendance records the employees concerned will have to keep job time records, either a card or slip for each job on which they work or a daily or weekly timesheet listing the various jobs. Such records should be scrutinised and approved by a supervisor or other manager. When a bonus system is in operation, the record will also show the time allowed for each job.

The accounts department will reconcile the job time bookings for a period with the recorded attendance times, any discrepancy being investigated.

After reconciliation, the various job hours will be summarised and valued at gross pay rates.

1.6 Wages analysis sheet

A wages analysis sheet will be used to split the wages costs between each job. A typical wages analysis sheet is given below.

Example

WAGES ANALYSIS SHEET

Department: Assembly   Week ended: 17.5.XX

Average hourly rate: £5.25

Employee	Production work								Non-productive			Total hours
Clock no	Jo no 10		Job no 15		Job no 17		Job no 21					
	Hrs	£	Hrs	£	Hrs	£	Hrs	£	Code	Hrs	£	
1214	12	63.00							107	4	21.00	40
1215			8	42.00	15	78.75	16	84.00				40
1216	30	157.50	15	78.75			10	52.50				40
1217	25	131.25	10	52.50	8	42.00			102	7	36.75	40
1218			12	63.00	20	105.00	4	21.00	107	4	21.00	40
Total hours	67		45		43		30			15		200
Total amount		351.75		236.25		225.75		157.50			78.75	1,050.00

The wages cost of each employee for each job is recorded on the job card.

1.7 Overhead costs

In just the same way as overheads are absorbed into cost units in an absorption costing system, so the overheads must also be absorbed into each job in a job costing system. This absorption will be done according to the absorption basis that the business uses, probably either on a direct labour hour basis or a machine hour basis.

Activity 1

Given below are the direct costs of job number 3362.

	£
Materials requisitions:	
15496	1,044
15510	938
15525	614
Wages analysis:	
Employee 13249 40 hours	320
Employee 12475 33 hours	231
Employee 26895 53 hours	312

Overheads are apportioned to jobs at the rate of £3.50 per direct labour hour.

What is the total cost of Job 3362?

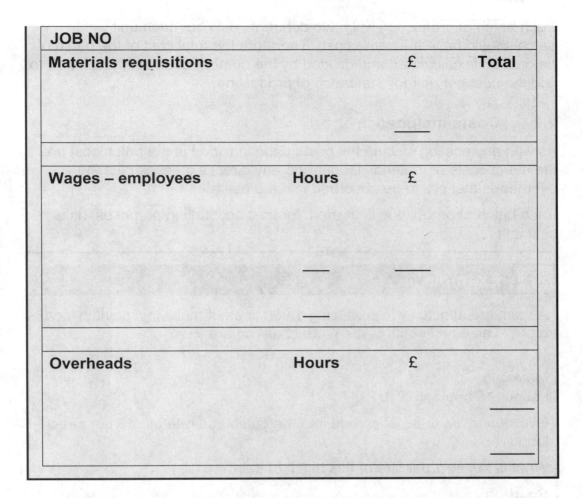

JOB NO			
Materials requisitions		**£**	**Total**
		———	
Wages – employees	**Hours**	**£**	
	——	——	
	——		
Overheads	**Hours**	**£**	
		———	
		———	

The principles behind a job costing system are exactly the same as those in a unit costing system with the job being treated as the cost unit. What a job costing system does mean is that there must be tight control over the coding of all materials requisitions and hours worked to ensure that each job is charged with the correct direct costs and eventually overheads.

2 Batch costing

2.1 Introduction

Batch costing is suitable for a business that produces batches of identical units, but each batch is for different units.

For example, a clothing manufacturer may have a production run for a batch of men's white shirts of collar size 16 inches. It may then have a production run for a batch of men's trousers with a waist size of 34 inches.

Each batch of production will have different costs but each unit within the batch should have the same cost. Therefore the total cost of the batch of production is calculated and divided by the number of units in that batch to find the cost per unit for that batch of production.

2.2 Costs included

As with any costing system the costs to be included in the batch cost are the direct costs of material, labour and any direct expenses plus the overheads that are to be absorbed into the batch.

Each batch of production is treated, for cost accounting purposes, as a cost unit.

 Example

A paint manufacturer is producing 1,000 litres of matt vinyl paint in 'sea blue'. The direct costs of the production run are:

	£
Materials	1,600
Labour 15 hours @ £10	150

Overheads are to be absorbed into the batch at a rate of £16 per direct labour hour.

What is the cost per litre of this batch of paint?

Solution

Batch cost	£
Materials	1,600
Labour	150
Overheads 15 hours @ £16	240
	———
Total batch cost	1,990
	———
Cost per litre =	1,000
=	£1.99

Activity 2

A manufacturer of frozen meals produces a batch of 20,000 units of salmon tagliatelli. The direct costs of this batch are:

	£
Materials	15,000
Labour 1,000 hours	4,200

Overheads are to be absorbed at rate of £1.20 per direct labour hour.

The cost of each portion of salmon tagliatelli is?

A   £1.20

B   £0.96

C   £2.16

D   £1.02

3 Summary

In this short chapter we have considered different costing systems that are suitable for different types of organisation.

A business that produces **one-off products** for customers, each of which is different, will use a **job costing** system. This treats each individual job as a cost unit and therefore attributes the direct costs to that job, as well as the overheads according to the organisation's overhead absorption basis.

In a business which produces a number of different products but produces them in **batches of an identical unit** then a **batch costing** system is appropriate. Here the costs of each batch of production are gathered together as though the batch was a cost unit and the actual cost per unit is calculated by dividing the batch cost by the number of units produced in that batch.

Answers to chapter activities

Activity 1

JOB NO	3362		
Materials requisitions		£	**Total**
15496		1,044	
15510		938	
15525		614	
		——	
			2,596

Wages – employees	**Hours**	£	
13249	40	320	
12475	33	231	
26895	53	312	
	——	——	
	126		863
	——		

Overheads	**Hours**	£	
Absorption rate £12	126	441	441
			——
Total cost			3,900
			——

Activity 2

Answer D

	£
Materials	15,000
Labour	4,200
Overheads 1,000 hours @ £1.2	1,200
Total cost	20,400
Cost per unit	20,400
	20,000
=	£1.02

Process costing

Introduction

In this chapter we are going to look at a costing system known as process costing. This type of costing is used when goods or services result from a sequence of continuous or repetitive operations or processes, for example in the manufacture of paint.

KNOWLEDGE

Explain the relationship between the various costing and accounting systems within an organisation (1.2)

Identify the most appropriate costing system (2.6)

- job
- batch
- unit
- process
- service

Recognise stock in its various stages (2.7):

- raw materials
- part-finish goods (work in progress)
- finished goods

SKILLS

Record and analyse costs in accordance with the organisation's costing procedures (1.1)

CONTENTS

1 Basics of process costing
2 Losses in processing
3 Scrap value of losses
4 Accounting for normal loss, abnormal loss and gain
5 Equivalent units and closing work-in-progress
6 Opening work-in-progress

1 Basics of process costing

1.1 Introduction

Process costing is the costing method applicable where goods or services result from a **sequence of continuous** or repetitive operations or **processes**. Process costing is used when a company is **mass producing** the same item and the item goes through a number of different stages.

Process costing is sometimes referred to as continuous operation costing.

Examples include the chemical, cement, oil, paint and textile industries.

1.2 Illustration of process costing

Here is an example of a two-process manufacturing operation:

HYRA has a manufacturing operation that involves two processes. The data for the first process during a particular period is as follows:

- At the beginning of the period, 2,500 kg materials are introduced to the process at a cost of £3,500.

- These materials are then worked upon, using £600 of labour and incurring/absorbing £450 of overheads.

The resulting output is passed to the second process.

To keep track of the costs we could prepare a process account for each process. This resembles a **T account with extra columns**. The reason for the extra columns is that we have to keep track of how many units we are working on as well as their value.

The costs appearing in such an account are those for **materials, labour and overheads**. (Labour and overheads are often combined under the heading 'conversion costs'.) In the case of **materials we record both units and monetary amount**; in the case of conversion costs we record the monetary amount only, because they do not add any units.

With process accounts the **inputs** into the process go into the **left** (debit) side of the account and **output** on the **right** (credit) side.

-Ọ́- **Example**

The process account for the above example might thus appear as follows.

Process 1 account

	Kg	£		Kg	£
Materials	2,500	3,500	Output		
Labour		600	materials to		
Overheads		450	Process 2	2,500	4,550
	2,500	4,550		2,500	4,550

1.3 The basic process cost per unit

Process costing is very similar to batch costing, as we calculate the total costs for the process and divide by the number of units to get a cost per unit.

The main difference is that the process is ongoing so the costs and output for a particular time period are used.

Using the example above we can calculate the cost per kg of output that will be transferred to the second process:

The calculation that needs to be done:

$$\text{Cost per unit} = \frac{\text{Net costs of input}}{\text{Expected output}}$$

Net costs of input   =   £3,500 + £600 + £450 = £4,550

Expected output   =   2,500 kg

Thus, the output to process 2 would be costed at:

$$\frac{£4,550}{2,500 \text{ kg}} = £1.82 \text{ per kg output}$$

2 Losses in process

2.1 Introduction

In many industrial processes, some input is lost (through evaporation, wastage, etc) or damaged during the production process. This will give rise to losses in the process. We will look at the concepts of normal losses and abnormal losses or gains.

Normal loss represents items that you **expect** to lose during a process, and its cost is therefore treated as part of the cost of good production. **Abnormal losses or gains** are **not expected** so are valued at the same cost as good production.

2.2 Normal Losses

Normal losses are usually stated as a percentage of input i.e. the normal loss is expected to be 5% of the input material. Unless the normal loss can be sold as scrap the cost of the loss is absorbed into the production cost.

Example

At the start of a heating process 1,000kg of material costing £16 per kg is input. During the process, conversion costs of £2,000 are incurred. Normal loss (through evaporation) is expected to be 10% of input. During March 1,000kg were input and output was 900kg.

Compute the unit and total cost of output in March.

Solution

First we need to sort out the units. We can do this using the flow of units equation:

Input		=>	Output	+	Loss
1,000 kg		=>	900 kg	+	100 kg (to balance)

The normal loss is 10% of input = 100kg thus the loss was as expected i.e. it is all normal loss.

We now need to compute the cost per unit of good output.

Total input costs:

Materials	£16 × 1,000 kg	£16,000
Conversion costs		£2,000
		————
		£18,000
		————

These costs will be spread over the good output units – thus the cost attributable to the normal loss units is absorbed into the good units.

Cost per unit of output:

$$= \frac{\text{Net costs of input}}{\text{Expected output}}$$

Where the expected output is now the input units less the normal loss units

$$= \frac{£18,000}{(1,000 - 100)}$$

$$= \quad £20 \text{ per kg}$$

Total cost of output = 900 kg × £20 = £18,000.

This can be represented in a process account as follows.

Process account – March

	Kg	£		Kg	£
Input	1,000	16,000	Output	900	18,000
Conversion costs	–	2,000	Normal loss	100	–
	———	———		———	———
	1,000	18,000		1,000	18,000
	———	———		———	———

Notice that the units and the monetary amounts balance. Normal loss is valued at zero as its cost has been absorbed into that of good output.

2.2 Abnormal loss

Any actual **loss in excess of the normal** (expected) loss is known as **abnormal loss**. This is not treated as part of normal production cost and is separately identified and costed throughout the process.

 Example

In April, 1,000 kg were input (at £16 per kg) to the same process as above and actual output was 800 kg. Conversion costs were £2,000 as before.

Required

Prepare the process account for the month of April.

Solution

Again look at the units only to start with.

Input	**= >**	**Output**	**+**	**Loss**
1,000 kg	= >	800 kg	+	200 kg (to balance)

The total loss is now 200 kg, when we only expected a (normal) loss of 100 kg.

Input	**= >**	**Output**	**+**	**Normal Loss**	**+**	**Abnormal Loss**
1,000 kg	= >	800 kg	+	100 kg	+	100kg

The extra 100 kg is an abnormal loss. It represents items that we did not expect to lose. In this example it may have been that the temperature was set too high on the process, causing more of the input to evaporate.

To make the units balance we therefore need to include 100 units on the right of the process account to represent this abnormal loss:

Process account – April (units only)

	Kg	£		Kg	£
Input	1,000		Output	800	
Conversion costs	–		Normal loss	100	
			Abnormal loss	100	
	1,000			1,000	

KAPLAN PUBLISHING

Now we examine the costs:

Cost per unit of output

$$= \frac{\text{Net costs of input}}{\text{Expected output}}$$

Where the expected output is the input units less the normal loss units, we were not expecting to have any extra loss

$$= \frac{\pounds18,000}{(1,000 - 100)}$$

$$= \quad \pounds20 \text{ per kg}$$

Total cost of output = 900 kg × £20 = £18,000.

This can be represented in a process account as follows.

Input, normal loss and output are valued at the same cost per kg as before. The value for abnormal loss is the same as that of output, i.e. £20 per kg.

Process account – April

	Kg	£		Kg	£
Input	1,000	16,000	Output	800	16,000
Conversion			Normal loss	100	-
costs	–	2,000	Abnormal loss	100	2,000
	1,000	18,000		1,000	18,000

The units and values are now balanced. The £2,000 value of the abnormal loss represents lost output.

2.3 Abnormal gain

An **abnormal gain** occurs where **losses are less than expected**. Its treatment is the same as abnormal loss only the debits and credits are reversed i.e. the gain is a debit in the t-account.

 Example

In May 1,000 kg at £16 per kg were input to the heating process and £2,000 conversion costs incurred. This month output was 950 kg.

Required

Prepare the process account for the month of May.

Solution

We begin by looking at the units flow.

Input	**= >**	**Output**	**+**	**Loss**
1,000 kg	= >	950 kg	+	50 kg (to balance)

The total loss is now only 50 kg, when we expected a (normal) loss of 1,000 × 10% = 100 kg. We have therefore made an abnormal gain of 50 kg

To balance the units on the process account then, we need to put the normal loss (100 kg) on the right and the abnormal gain (50 kg) on the left.

Abnormal Gain	**+**	**Input**	**= >**	**Output**	**+**	**Normal Loss**
50kg	+	1,000 kg	= >	950 kg	+	100 kg

Now we examine the costs:
Cost per unit of output:

$$= \frac{\text{Net costs of input}}{\text{Expected output}}$$

Where the expected output is the input units less the normal loss units, we were not expecting the loss to be any different.

$$= \frac{£18,000}{(1,000 - 100)}$$

$$= £20 \text{ per kg}$$

Total cost of output = 900 kg × £20 = £18,000.

This can be represented in a process account as follows. Input, normal loss and output are valued at the same cost per kg as before. The value for abnormal gain is the same as that of output, i.e. £20 per kg. The completed process account is shown below.

Process account – May

	Kg	£		Kg	£
Input	1,000	16,000	Output	950	19,000
Conversion costs	–	2,000	Normal loss	100	–
Abnormal gain	50	1,000			
	1,050	19,000		1,050	19,000

The abnormal gain has to go on the left to avoid having negative numbers in the T account.

We have an additional 50 units to sell at £20 per unit.

 Activity 1

You are given the following information about the 'mashing' process of Mushypeas Ltd during June:

Ingredients input	1,600 kg @ £2.80 per kg
Labour	100 hours @ £6 per hour
Overheads	100 hours @ £3.60 per hour

Actual Output from the process is 1,250kg

Water loss from the process is expected to result in a 15% loss in input volume.

Calculate the cost per kg of output and use it to complete the mashing process account below

Solution

Process A

	Kg	unit cost	£		Kg	unit cost	£
Ingredients	1,600	2.80		Normal Loss		0.00	
Labour		6.00		Output	1,250		
Overheads		3.60					
	——	——			——	——	
	——	——			——	——	

Use the following phases and numbers to complete the above t-account:

Abnormal Loss	Abnormal Gain	9,600
5,760	5,000	4,480
600	440	360
240	110	4.35
4.00	5,440	

3 Scrap value of losses

3.1 Introduction

It may be possible to **sell** the **normal** loss that occurs from a process as a side product of the process for example wood shavings as a side product of making wooden tables and chairs.

 Example

Maine Ltd produces tables and chairs. When they are produced wood shavings are produced. These wood shavings are saved and sold off for 90p/kg. Normal waste is 10% of input. Costs for batch 975D were as follows.

	£
Materials (10,000 kg @ £2 per kg)	20,000
Labour	2,000
Overheads	500
Total	22,500
Actual output	8,500 kg

Required

Prepare the process account.

Solution

First, the units:

Input	=>	Output	+	Loss
10,000 kg	=>	8,500 kg	+	1,500 kg (to balance)

The total loss is 1,500 kg, when we only expected a (normal) loss of 10% × 10,000 = 1,000 kg. Thus, we have an abnormal loss of 500 kg.

Input	=>	Output	+	Normal Loss	+	Abnormal Loss
10,000 kg	=>	8,500 kg	+	1,000 kg	+	500kg

In this example we would sell the normal loss at £900 (1,000kg @ £0.90 = £900). This is entered in the process account. The same amount is then subtracted from the process costs, reducing the cost of the inputs i.e. to the net cost of inputs.

$$\text{Cost per unit} = \frac{\text{Net costs of input}}{\text{Expected output}}$$

$$\text{Cost per unit} = \frac{£22,500 - £900}{10,000 - 1,000} = £2.40 \text{ per kg}$$

Although we actually have 1,500 loss units to sell (1,000 litres of normal loss plus 500 units of abnormal loss), we only include the sales value of the normal loss in this calculation as this is all we were expecting to sell.

Process account

	Kg	£		Kg	£
Input	10,000	20,000	Output @ £2.40	8,500	20,400
Material Labour	–	2,000	Normal loss		
Overheads	500		@ £0.90	1,000	900
			Abnormal loss		
			@ £2.40	500	1,200
	10,000	22,500		10,000	22,500

 Activity 2

Y plc runs a distillery making whisky. Input to a batch was as follows.

	£
Materials (1,000 litres)	5,000
Labour and overheads	427
Total	5,427

Normal loss is 10% of input as impurities are removed.

Actual output = 920 litres. The impurities were sold for 27p per litre.

Required

Complete the process account below

Process account

	Ltr	unit cost	£		Ltr	unit cost	£
Material Conversion				Normal Loss Output			

Activity 3

A chemical compound is made by raw material being processed through two processes. The output of Process A is passed to Process B where further material is added to the mix. The details of the process costs for the financial period number 10 were as shown below.

Process A

Direct materials	2,000 kg @ £5 per kg
Direct labour	£7,200
Process plant time	140 hours @ £60 per hour

Process B

Input from process A	?
Direct material	1,400 kg @ £12 per kg
Direct labour	£4,200
Process plant time	80 hours @ £72.50 per hour

The departmental overhead for period 10 was £6,840 and is absorbed into the costs of each process on direct labour costs in each process.

	Process A	Process B
Expected output	80% of input	90% of input
Actual output	1,400 kg	2,620 kg

Normal loss is contaminated material, which is sold as scrap for £0.50 per kg from Process A and £1.825 per kg from Process B.

Required

Prepare the process accounts below:

Process account – Process A

	Kg	unit cost	£		Kg	unit cost	£
Material				Normal Loss			
Conversion				Output			
	___		___		___		___
	___		___		___		___

Process account – Process B

	Kg	unit cost	£		Kg	unit cost	£
Material				Normal Loss			
Conversion				Output			
	___		___		___		___
	___		___		___		___

4 Accouting for normal loss, abnormal loss and gain

4.1 Normal loss

Normal loss, if it has a scrap value, reduces the cost of production and is recorded in the process account as a credit. The debit side of this transaction occurs in a **normal loss account** (1). The money received for the normal loss is recorded in the cash or bank account.

Example

Stardust Ltd produces wooden ceiling decorations. When they are produced wood shavings are also produced. These wood shavings are saved and sold off for 50p/kg. Normal loss is 5% of input. Costs for batch 13 were as follows.

	£
Materials (20,000 kg @ £2 per kg)	40,000
Labour	4,000
Overheads	1,000
Total	45,000
Actual output	19,000 kg

Solution

Input	=>	Output	+	Normal Loss
20,000 kg	=>	19,000 kg	+	1,000 kg

$$\text{Cost per unit} = \frac{£45,000 - £500}{20,000 - 1,000} = £2.3421 \text{ per kg}$$

Process account

	£		£
Materials	40,000	Normal loss (1)	500
Conversion	5,000	Output	44,500
	45,000		45,000

Normal loss account

	£		£
Process (1)	500	Cash	500
	500		500

4.2 Abnormal losses

Abnormal losses are valued at the **cost of production** in the **process account** to reflect the lost good output. These values are recorded in the **process account** as a **credit** and the **abnormal loss account** as a **debit** (2).

If normal losses can be sold, this **extra loss** can then also be **sold for cash.** To record this transaction we **credit the abnormal loss account** with the value of the abnormal loss units **sold at the scrap value** (the price the normal loss was sold at) and **debit** in the **normal loss account** (3). The will increase the amount of money received that is recorded in the cash or bank account.

The final stage is to find out how much the **abnormal loss really cost** the business. This is done by **balancing the abnormal loss account** and the balancing figure will then go as a **debit (expense)** in the **profit and loss** account (4).

If normal losses cannot be sold the value of the abnormal loss in the process account is debited straight to the profit and loss account.

☼ Example

Stardust Ltd produces wooden ceiling decorations. When they are produced wood shavings are also produced. These wood shavings are saved and sold off for 50p/kg. Normal loss is 5% of input. Costs for batch 13 were as follows.

	£
Materials (20,000 kg @ £2 per kg)	40,000
Labour	4,000
Overheads	1,000
Total	45,000
Actual output	18,000 kg

Solution

Input	=>	Output	+	Normal Loss	+	Abnormal Loss
20,000 kg	=>	18,000 kg	+	1,000 kg	+	1,000kg

$$\text{Cost per unit} = \frac{£45,000 - £500}{20,000 - 1,000} = £2.3421 \text{ per kg}$$

Process account

	£		£
Materials	40,000	Normal loss (1)	500
Conversion	5,000	Output	42,158
		Abnormal loss (2)	2,342
	———		———
	45,000		45,000
	———		———

Normal loss account

	£		£
Process (1)	500	Cash	1,000
Abnormal loss (3)	500		
	———		———
	1,000		1,000
	———		———

Abnormal loss account

	£		£
Process (2)	2,342	Normal loss (3)	500
		Profit and loss (4)	1,842
	———		———
	2,342		2,342
	———		———

4.3 Abnormal Gains

Abnormal gains are valued at the **cost of production** in the **process account** to reflect the **unexpected reduction in losses.** These values are recorded in the **process account** as a **debit** and the **abnormal gain account** as a **credit** (2).

If normal losses can be sold, an abnormal gain will reduce the number of units of normal loss we have to sell. This **reduction to the normal loss** is recorded as a **debit in the abnormal gain account** with the value of the abnormal gain **units at the scrap value** (the price the normal loss was sold at) and a **credit** in the **normal loss account** (3). The cash figure is then the balancing amount in the account. An abnormal gain will decrease the amount of money received that is recorded in the cash or bank account.

The final stage is to find out how much extra income the abnormal gain has produced for the business. This is done by **balancing the abnormal gain account** and the balancing figure will then go as a **credit (income)** in the **profit and loss** account (4).

If normal losses cannot be sold the value of the abnormal gain in the process account is credited straight to the profit and loss account.

Example

Stardust Ltd produces wooden ceiling decorations. When they are produced wood shavings are also produced. These wood shavings are saved and sold off for 50p/kg. Normal loss is 5% of input. Costs for batch 13 were as follows.

	£
Materials (20,000 kg @ £2 per kg)	40,000
Labour	4,000
Overheads	1,000
Total	45,000
Actual output	19,500 kg

Solution

Abnormal Gain	+	Input	=>	Output	+	Normal Loss
500	+	20,000 kg	=>	19,500 kg	+	1,000 kg

$$\text{Cost per unit} = \frac{£45,000 - £500}{20,000 - 1,000} = £2.3421 \text{ per kg}$$

Process account

	£		£
Materials	40,000	Normal loss (1)	500
Conversion	5,000	Output	45,671
Abnormal gain (2)	1,171		
	———		———
	46,171		46,171
	———		———

Normal loss account

	£		£
Process (1)	500	Cash	250
		Abnormal gain (3)	250
	———		———
	500		500
	———		———

Abnormal gain account

	£		£
Normal loss (3)	250	Process (2)	1,171
Profit and loss (4)	921		
	———		———
	1,171		1,171
	———		———

Activity 4

X plc processes a chemical. Input to a batch was as follows.

	£
Materials (10,000 litres)	10,000
Labour and overheads	800
	———
Total	10,800
	———

Normal loss is 10% of input.

Actual output = 8,700 litres. The remaining liquid was skimmed off and sold for 36p per litre.

Required

Complete the process account, normal loss account and abnormal loss or gain account.

Process account

	Ltr	unit cost	£		Ltr	unit cost	£
Material				Normal Loss			
Conversion				Output			
	———		———		———		———
	———		———		———		———

Normal loss account

	£		£
	_____		_____
	_____		_____

Abnormal loss/gain account

	£		£
	_____		_____
	_____		_____

5 Equivalent units and closing work-in-progress

5.1 Introduction

Process costing is also used when products **may not be completed at the end of a time period** (e.g. manufacturing cars). This means that the process costs are shared between finished or complete units and **work in progress or partially completed units.**

We need to decide how the costs should be split over these different categories of production. Note that you are only expected to deal with closing work-in-progress.

5.2 Equivalent Units

To be able to assign the correct amount of cost to finished and partially completed units of product we use a concept called Equivalent Units or EU. To demonstrate this concept:

If we had 1,000 units that are 50% complete at the end of a period. How many finished units is this equivalent to?

$1,000 \times 50\% = 500$ equivalent units (EU).

In other words, we assume we could have made 500 units and finished them instead of half finishing 1,000 units.

The calculation of equivalent units:

Equivalent units = Number of physical units × percentage completion

---

💡 Example

Situation A – CWIP completion levels are equal

DL Ltd is a manufacturer. In Period 1 the following production occurred.

Started   =   1,400

Closing work-in-progress

(abbreviated as CWIP)   =   400 units

Degree of completion for the CWIP:

    Materials   25%

    Conversion   25%

Solution

Started   = >   Finished   +   CWIP

1,400   = >   1,000 (to balance)   +   400

Finished units are 100% complete for both material and conversion.

	EUs		
Finished	1,000 × 100%		1,000
WIP	400 × 25%		100
Total			1,100

5.3   Equivalent Units for different degress of completion

A process involves direct materials being processed by the addition of direct labour and overheads.

Usually, all the material is put in at the beginning of the process, whereas the conversion is 'added' as the product advances through the process. This means there may be a **different amount of equivalent units for conversion and materials.**

If completion levels in the closing work in progress are unequal we have to keep track of the equivalent units for materials and for conversion separately.

Example

Situation B – completion levels are unequal

EM Ltd is a manufacturer. In Period 1 the following production occurred.

Started   =   1,400

Closing work-in-progress (abbreviated as CWIP) =   400 units

Degree of completion:
        Materials   100%
        Conversion   50%

Solution

Started   = >   Finished   +   CWIP

1,400   = >   1,000 (to balance) +   400

Finished units are 100% complete for both material and conversion.

			EUs
Materials	– Finished 1,000×100%		1,000
	– CWIP 400 × 100%		400
			1,400
Conversion	– Finished 1,000 × 100%		1,000
	– CWIP 400 × 50%		200
			1,200

5.4   Valuing work-in-progress and finished goods

We need to be able to calculate the cost of an equivalent unit to be able to value the cost of finished goods and closing WIP. We will first look at this was completion levels of the CWIP are equal.

 Example

Situation A continued – completion levels are equal

DL Ltd is a manufacturer. In Period 1 the following production occurred.
Started   =   1,400

Closing work-in-progress (abbreviated as CWIP) =   400 units

Degree of completion for the CWIP:

        Materials   25%

        Conversion   25%

Costs incurred in Period 1 = £6,600

Solution

Started	=>	Finished	+	CWIP
1,400	=>	1,000 (to balance)	+	400

Finished units are 100% complete for both material and conversion.

			EUs
Finished	1,000 × 100%		1,000
WIP	400 × 25%		100
			———
Total			1,100

The cost per equivalent unit is simply calculated as total cost divided by the number of EUs produced.

The cost per EU would be £6,600/1,100 = £6 per EU.

This can be used to calculate the value of the finished goods and closing WIP:

Value of finished units = 1,000 × £6 = £6,000

Value of closing WIP = 100 × £6 = £600

The process account for Period 1 would look as follows.

Process account

	£		£
Costs	6,600	Finished goods	6,000
		Closing WIP	600
	———		———
	6,600		6,600
	———		———

 Activity 5

Process WIP

On 1 March 20X0 a process started work on 350 units and at the end of the month there were still 75 units in the process, each 60% complete.

The total cost of materials, labour, etc input during March was £3,696.

Required

The value of the finished goods and CWIP is:

	Finished goods	CWIP
A	£3,176.25	£866.25
B	£1,155	£2,541
C	£3,176.25	£519.75
D	£1,155	£4,235

Now we need to look at calculating the cost of the finished goods and the CWIP when completion levels of the CWIP are unequal.

 Example

Situation B continued – completion levels are unequal

EM Ltd is a manufacturer. In Period 1 the following production occurred.

Started   = 1,400

Closing work-in-progress (abbreviated as CWIP)   =   400 units

Degree of completion:

    Materials   100%

    Conversion   50%

Costs incurred in Period 1:

    Materials   £81,060

    Conversion   £71,940

Solution

Started   = >   Finished   +   CWIP

1,400   = >   1,000 (to balance) +   400

Finished units are 100% complete for both material and conversion.

		EUs
Materials	– Finished 1,000×100%	1,000
	– CWIP 400 × 100%	400
Conversion	– Finished 1,000 × 100%	1,000
	– CWIP 400 × 50%	200

Put the EU and costs into the table below

Input	Equivalent units			Costs	
	Completed in period EU	CWIP EU	Total EU	Total costs (£)	Costs per EU (£)
Materials	1,000	400 (100%)	1,400	81,060	57.90
Conversion	1,000	200 (50%)	1,200	71,940	59.95
				153,000	**117.85**

Total costs are then divided by the total EU to get a cost per EU for each type of input cost, and a total cost for each completed unit.

The costs may now be attributed to the categories of output as follows:

		£	£
Completed units:	1,000 × £117.85		117,850
Closing WIP:	Materials 400 × £57.90	23,160	
	Conversion 200 × £59.95	11,990	
			35,150
			153,000

The process account would appear as follows:

Process account

	£		£
Materials	81,060	Completed goods	117,850
Conversion	71,940	Closing WIP	35,150
	153,000		153,000

Activity 6

NH Ltd

NH Ltd has two processes.

Material for 12,000 items was put into process 1. There were no opening stocks and no process losses. Other relevant information is:

Transfers to process 2   9,000 items
Direct material cost   £36,000
Direct labour cost   £32,000
Overheads   £8,530

The unfinished items were complete as to materials and 50% complete as to labour and overheads. Information for process 2 is as follows:

Transfers from process 1 9,000 items (at a cost determined above)

Items completed   8,200 items

Labour cost   £34,596

Overheads   £15,300

There were no materials added in process 2 other than the units transferred from process 1. There were no process losses.

The unfinished items were deemed to be 25% complete in labour and overheads

Required

Prepare the process accounts below:

Process account 1

	£		£
Materials		Output to	
Labour		Process 2	
Overheads		CWIP	
	———		———
	———		———

Process account 2			
	£		£
Input from Process 1 Labour Overheads		Finished goods CWIP	
	_____		_____
	_____		_____

6   Opening work in progress (OWIP)

6.1   Introduction

At the start of a period there may be some work in progress from a previous period (closing work in progress) that is waiting to be finished. This is the known as the **opening work in progress (OWIP)** in the new period.

The OWIP needs to be considered to be able to calculate how much of the completed output at the end of the period was completed wholly in the period and how much only required partial effort to complete it within the period.

There are 2 different methods that can be applied to OWIP – First in, first out (FIFO) and Average cost (AVCO).

6.2   Average cost (AVCO)

The average cost method would be used where it is not possible to distinguish individual units present at the start of a process from those produced during the period i.e. liquids. In this case the **costs incurred so far to complete the OWIP are included with the period costs when calculating the cost per EU.**

Example

Than Pele

Than Pele Ltd is a manufacturer. The details of the first process in Period 2 are as follows:

OWIP	= 400 units
Costs incurred so far	
Materials	£19,880
Conversion	£3,775

Completed output	= 1,700 units

CWIP	= 300 units

Degree of completion:

Materials	100%
Conversion	50%

Costs incurred in Period 1:

Materials	£81,060
Conversion	£71,940

Solution

OWIP	+	Started	= >	Finished	+	CWIP
400	+	1,600	= >	1,700	+	300

Equivalent units		Material	Conversion
	Completed Output	1,700	1,700
	CWIP	300	150
	Total EU	2,000	1,850
Costs			
	OWIP	19,880	3,775
	Period	100,000	86,000
	Total cost	119,880	89,775
Cost per EU		£59.94	£48.53

The costs may now be attributed to the categories of output as follows:

		£	£
Completed units:	1,700 × (£59.94 + £48.53)		184,399
Closing WIP:	Materials 300 × £59.94	17,982	
	Conversion 150 × £48.53	7,279	
			25,261
			209,660

The process account would appear as follows:

Process account

	£		£
OWIP	23,655	Completed goods	184,399
Materials	100,000	Closing WIP	25,261
Conversion	86,000		
Rounding	5		
	209,660		209,660

 Activity 7

Yeknom

Yeknom produces a diet drink on a production line. The details of the process in Period 7 are as follows:

OWIP	=	200 units
Costs incurred so far		
Materials	£22,000	
Conversion	£9,960	
Completed output	=	900 units
CWIP	=	300 units
Degree of completion:		
Materials	100%	
Conversion	60%	

Costs incurred in Period 1:

| Materials | £98,000 |
| Conversion | £99,000 |

Complete the process accounting using the AVCO method of valuing OWIP

Solution

Equivalent units	Material	Conversion
Completed Output		
CWIP		
Total EU		

Costs

OWIP	
Period	
Total cost	

Cost per EU

The costs may now be attributed to the categories of output as follows:

	£	£

Completed units:

Closing WIP: Materials
Conversion

The process account would appear as follows:

Process account

	£		£
OWIP		Completed goods	
Materials		Closing WIP	
Conversion			

6.3   First in, first out (FIFO)

The first in, first out method would be used when it may be essential to complete the started goods from previous periods before new units can be started i.e. car production lines. In this case we need to consider **how much work is required to complete the OWIP. The costs incurred in the previous period for the OWIP are included within the valuation of the completed output.**

 Example

Than Pele

Than Pele Ltd is a manufacturer. The details of the first process in Period 2 are as follows:

OWIP	= 400 units

Costs incurred so far

Materials	£19,880
Conversion	£3,775

Degrees of completion

Materials	100%
Conversion	25%

Completed output	= 1,700 units

CWIP	= 300 units

Degree of completion:

Materials	100%
Conversion	50%

Costs incurred in Period 1:

Materials	£81,060
Conversion	£71,940

Solution

OWIP	+	Started	= >	Completed	+	CWIP
400	+	1,600	= >	1,700	+	300

The completed units consist of 400 OWIP that were completed this period and then a further 1,300 units that were started and finished in this period.

To complete the OWIP no more material is required but 75% more conversion is needed.

Equivalent units		Material	Conversion
	OWIP to complete	0 (400 - 400 × 100%)	300 (400 – 400 × 25%)
	Completed Output	1,300	1,300
	CWIP	300	150
	Total EU	1,600	1,750
Costs			
	Period	100,000	86,000
	Total cost	100,000	86,000
Cost per EU			
		£62.50	£49.14

The costs may now be attributed to the categories of output as follows:

		£	£
Completed units:	OWIP from previous period	23,655	
	OWIP completed	14,742	
	Completed output	145,132	
			183,529
Closing WIP:	Materials 300 × £59.94	17,982	
	Conversion 150 × £48.53	7,279	
			26,121
			209,650

The process account would appear as follows:

Process account

	£		£
OWIP	23,655	Completed goods	183,529
Materials	100,000	Closing WIP	26,121
Conversion	86,000	Rounding	5
	209,655		209,655

Activity 8

Effarig

Effarig is makes safari hats on a production line. The details of the process in Period 3 are as follows:

OWIP		=	200 units
Costs incurred so far			
Materials		£1,800	
Conversion		£4,000	
Degrees of completion			
Materials	100%		
Conversion	75%		

Completed output	=	2,000 units

CWIP	=	100 units
Degree of completion:		
Materials	100%	
Conversion	50%	

Costs incurred in Period 1:

Materials	£19,000
Conversion	£38,000

Complete the process accounting using the FIFO method of valuing OWIP

Solution

Equivalent units	Material	Conversion
OWIP to complete		
Completed Output		
CWIP		
Total EU		
Costs		
Period		
Total cost		
Cost per EU		

The costs may now be attributed to the categories of output as follows:

		£	£
Completed units:	OWIP from previous period		
	OWIP completed		
	Completed output		
Closing WIP:	Materials		
	Conversion		

The process account would appear as follows:

Process account

	£		£
OWIP		Completed goods	
Materials		Closing WIP	
Conversion			

7 Summary

As you now know, process costing is used when a company is mass producing the same item and the item goes through a number of different stages. As the item goes through the different stages, **losses** may occur: normal losses, abnormal losses and abnormal gains. Losses may be scrapped or they may have a '**scrap value**' which means that they can be sold (and that the revenue generated is used to reduce the costs of the process concerned).

Sometimes, at the end of an accounting period, a process may not be finished and there may be incomplete (**work-in-progress**) units. When this happens, it is necessary to use the concept of **equivalent units** to decide how the process costs should be split over work-in-progress and finished goods.

Test your knowledge

Having completed Chapter 8 you should now be able to attempt:

Practice Activities 26, 27, 28, 29, 30, 31, 32, 33 and 34

Answers to chapter activities

 Activity 1

Actual output = 1,250 kg

Flow of units:

Input   = >   Output   +   Loss

1,600 kg = >   1,250 kg   +   350 kg (to balance)

Normal loss = 240 kg and we therefore have an abnormal loss of 110 kg.

Process costs = £5,440

$$\text{Cost per unit of output} = \frac{\text{Total process costs}}{\text{Input units} - \text{Normal loss units}}$$

$$= \frac{£5,440}{(1,600 - 240)}$$

$$= £4 \text{ per kg, as before}$$

The process account will now look like this:

Mashing process – June

	kg	£		kg	£
Ingredients	1,600	4,480	Output	1,250	5,000
Labour		600	Normal loss	240	–
Overheads		360	Abnormal	110	440
	1,600	5,440		1,600	5,440

KAPLAN PUBLISHING

Activity 2

Y plc

Process account

	Ltrs	£		Ltrs	£
Input material	1,000	5,000	Output	920	5,520
Labour and overheads	–	427	Normal loss	100	27
Abnormal gain	20	120			
	1,020	5,547		1,020	5,547

Output valued at (£5,427 – £27)/900 = £6.00 per litre

Activity 3

Chemical compound

Process A

	kg	£		kg	£ per kg	£
Direct material	2,000	10,000	Normal loss (W2)	400	0.500	200
Direct labour		7,200	To Process B (W3)	1,400	18.575	26,005
Process costs		8,400	Abnormal loss	200	18.575	3,715
Overhead (W1)		4,320				
	2,000	29,920		2,000		29,920

(W1) £6,840 × 7,200/(7,200 + 4,200) = £4,320

(W2) Normal loss = 20% of input = 2,000 × 20% = 400 kg

(W3) Value of output = £(29,920 – 200)/(2,000 – 400) = £18.575 per kg

Process B

From	kg	£		kg	£ per kg	£
Process A	1,400	26,005	Finished goods (W6)	2,620	21.7516	56,989
Direct material	1,400	16,800	Normal loss (W4)	280	1.825	511
Direct labour		4,200				
Overhead		2,520				
Process costs		5,800				
		———				
Total costs		55,325				
Abnormal gain (W5, W6)	100	2,175				
	———	———		———		———
	2,900	57,500		2,900		57,500
	———	———		———		———

(W4) Normal loss = 10% × (1,400 + 1,400) = 280

(W5) Expected output = 2,800 − 280 = 2,520 units; actual output 2,620; 100 units abnormal gain

(W6) Cost per unit = £(55,325 − 511) / (2,800 − 280) = £21.7516 (kept this accurate to avoid rounding errors)

Activity 4

X plc

Process account

	Ltrs	£		Ltrs	£
Input material	10,000	10,000	Output	8,700	10,092
Labour and overheads	–	800	Normal loss	1,000	360
			Abnormal loss	300	348
	———	———		———	———
	10,000	10,800		10,000	10,800
	———	———		———	———

Output valued at (£10,800 − £360)/9,000 = £1.16 per litre

Normal loss account

	£		£
Process	360	Cash	468
Abnormal loss	108		
	———		———
	468		468
	———		———

Abnormal loss account

	£		£
Process	348	Normal loss	108
		Profit and loss	240
	_____		_____
	348		348
	_____		_____

Activity 5

Answer C

Physical flow of units

Units started		Units completed		Closing WIP
350	=	275 (bal fig)	+	75

Equivalent units of production

Units started and finished	275
Closing WIP (75 × 60%)	45
	_____
	320
	_____

$$\text{Cost per equivalent unit} = \frac{£3,696}{320} = £11.55$$

Value of finished goods =	275 × £11.55	=	£3,176.25
Value of closing WIP =	45 × £11.55	=	£519.75
			_____
			£3,696
			_____

Activity 6

NH Ltd

Process 1

The physical flow of units:

Units started	=	Units completed	+	Closing WIP
12,000	=	9,000	+	3,000 (bal)

Input	Effective units			Costs	Costs per EU (£)
	Completed in period	CWIP	Total EU	Total costs (£)	
Materials	9,000	3,000 (100%)	12,000	36,000	3.00
Conversion	9,000	1,500 (50%)	10,500	40,530	3.86
				76,530	**6.86**

The costs may now be attributed to the categories of output as follows:

		£	£
Completed units	9,000 × £6.86		61,740
Closing WIP:	Materials 3,000 × £3	9,000	
	Conversion 1,500 × £3.86	5,790	
			14,790
			76,530

The process account will thus appear as follows:

Process 1 account

	Units	£		Units	£
Materials	12,000	36,000	Process 2	9,000	61,740
Labour		32,000	Work-in-		
Overheads		8,530	progress	3,000	14,790
		76,530			76,530

Process 2

The physical flow of units:

Units started = Units completed + Closing WIP
  9,000   =   8,200   +   800 (bal)

Input	Completed in period	CWIP	Total EU	Total costs (£)	Costs per EU (£)
Process 1	8,200	800 (100%)	9,000	61,740	6.86
Conversion	8,200	200 (25%)	8,400	49,896	5.94
				111,636	**12.80**

The costs may now be attributed to the categories of output as follows:

		£	£
Completed units	8,200 × £12.80		104,960
Closing WIP:	Process 1 800 × £6.86	5,488	
	Conversion 200 x £5.94	1,188	
			6,676
			111,636

The process account will thus appear as follows:

Process 2 account

	Units	£		Units	£
Materials (process 1)	9,000	61,740	Finished goods	8,200	104,960
Labour		34,596	Work-in-process	800	6,676
Overheads		15,300			
	9,000	111,636		9,000	111,636

Activity 7

Equivalent units		Material	Conversion
	Completed Output	900	900
	CWIP	300	180
	Total EU	1,200	1,080
Costs			
	OWIP	22,000	9,960
	Period	98,000	99,000
	Total cost	120,000	108,960
Cost per EU		£100	£100.89

The costs may now be attributed to the categories of output as follows:

		£	£
Completed units:	Completed output	180,801	
			180,801
Closing WIP:	Materials 300 × £100	30,000	
	Conversion 180 × £100.89	18,160	
			48,160
			228,961

The process account would appear as follows:

Process account

	£		£
OWIP	31,960	Completed goods	59,090
Materials	98,000	Closing WIP	48,160
Conversion	99,000		
Rounding	1		
	228961		228,961

Activity 8

OWIP   +   Started   = >   Completed   +   CWIP
200   +   1,900   = >   2000   +   100

The completed units consist of 200 OWIP that were completed this period and then a further 1,800 units that were started and finished in this period.

To complete the OWIP no more material is required but 25% more conversion is needed.

Equivalent units		Material	Conversion
	OWIP to complete	0 (200 - 200 × 100%)	50 (200 – 200 × 75%)
	Completed Output	1,800	1,800
	CWIP	300	50
	Total EU	2,100	1,900
Costs			
	Period	19,000	38,000
	Total cost	19,000	38,000
Cost per EU		£9.05	£20

The costs may now be attributed to the categories of output as follows:

		£	£
Completed units:	OWIP from previous period	5,800	
	OWIP completed	1,000	
	Completed output	52,290	
			59,090
Closing WIP:	Materials 300 × £9.05	2,715	
	Conversion 50 × £20	1,000	
			3,715
			62,805

The process account would appear as follows:

Process account

	£		£
OWIP	5,800	Completed goods	59,090
Materials	19,000	Closing WIP	3,715
Conversion	38,000		
Rounding	5		
	_____		_____
	62,805		62,805
	_____		_____

Basic variance analysis

9

Introduction

In this chapter we are going to look at how to produce basic budgets, why budgets differ from actual results and the variances that arise.

KNOWLEDGE

Explain the purpose of internal reporting and providing accurate information to management in terms of decision making, planning and control (1.1)

Explain the characteristics of different types of cost classifications and their use in costing (1.4)

Identify costs and the correct classification (2.2)

– fixed

– variable

– semi-variable

– stepped

Explain the effect of changing activity levels on unit costs (3.1)

SKILLS

Compare budget costs with actual costs and note any variances (3.1)

Analyse variances accurately and prepare relevant reports for management (3.2)

Inform budget holders and other managers of any significant variances; making valid suggestions for remedial action (3.3)

CONTENTS

1 Re-cap – cost behaviour and changing activity levels
2 Basic variance analysis
3 Reasons and solutions for variances

1 Recap – cost behaviour and activity levels

1.1 Variable costs

Variable costs increase in direct proportion to activity, i.e. as activity increases so do the costs. Variable costs are constant per unit.

Direct costs are assumed to be variable costs.

1.2 Fixed costs

Fixed costs are constant as activity increases. Fixed costs per unit decrease as activity increases.

1.3 Stepped costs

Stepped costs are fixed to a certain level of activity and then the cost steps up to a new fixed level.

1.4 Semi-variable costs

Semi-variable costs are costs that have a fixed and a variable element. The cost therefore increases as activity increases (the variable element) but will not have a zero cost at zero activity (the fixed element). The two parts of the cost can be separately calculated using the High-low method.

1.5 Sales revenue

Sales revenue is assumed to have a variable behaviour unless stated otherwise i.e. the more units that are sold the more revenue there is and there is a constant selling price per unit.

2 Basic variance analysis

2.1 Budgets

Budgets are prepared for number of reasons:

- To forecast future activity levels
- To communicate goals and objectives
- To plan for the use of resources – materials, labour, money

- To control the different departments

- To motivate by setting achieveable targets

These are the same as the aims of management accounting (chapter 1)

Budgets are produced in advance of production but are then compared to actual results at the end of a time period to enable analysis of each department to occur.

2.2 Flexed budgets

Problems can happen if actual production levels differ from the budgeted production levels. To overcome this issue budgets are flexed to match the actual production level.

Flexed budgets are produced using the cost behaviour principles re-capped above.

 Activity 1

Victor Ltd is preparing it's budget for the next quarter and it needs to consider different production levels.

The semi-variable costs should be calculated using the high-low method. If 3,000 batches are produced then the semi-variable cost will be £8,500.

Complete the table below and calculate the estimated profit per batch at the different activity levels.

Batches sold and produced	1,000	1,500	2,000
Sale Revenue	40,000		
Variable cost			
Direct Materials	4,000		
Direct Labour	3,800		
Overheads	7,200		
Semi-variable costs	4,500		
Variable element			
Fixed element			
Fixed cost	3,500		
Total cost	23,000		
Total profit	17,000		
Profit per batch (to 2 decimal places)	17.00		

2.3 Variances

Once a flexed budget is prepared for the appropriate activity level it is then possible to calculate the amount the actual figures differ from the budget i.e. the variance.

An **adverse** variance occurs when the **actual costs exceeds the budgeted costs** or when the **actual revenue is less than the budgeted revenue.**

A **favourable** variance occurs when the **actual cost is less than the budgeted cost** or when the **actual revenue exceeds the budgeted revenue.**

 Activity 2

Victor Ltd is preparing it's budget for the next quarter and it needs to consider different production levels. The semi-variable costs should be calculated using the high-low method.

If 3,000 batches are produced then the semi-variable cost will be £8,500.

Complete the table below and calculate the estimated profit per batch at the different activity levels.

	Budget	Actual
Volume Sold	1,000	1,400
	£	£
Sale Revenue	40,000	60,000
Less costs:		
Direct Materials	4,000	6,000
Direct Labour	3,800	5,300
Overheads	7,200	10,100
Semi-variable costs	4,500	5,500
Fixed cost	3,500	3,500
Total profit	17,000	29,600

Complete the table below to show a flexed budget and the resulting variances, indicating if it is a favourable (F) or adverse (A) in the final column.

	Flexed Budget	Actual	Variance value	Favourable or Adverse
Volume Sold		1,400		
	£	£	£	
Sale Revenue		60,000		
Less costs:				
Direct Materials		6,000		
Direct Labour		5,300		
Overheads		10,100		
Semi-variable costs		5,500		
Fixed cost		3,500		
Total profit		29,600		

3   Causes and solutions for variances

3.1 Introduction

There are a number of reasons for variances. You will need to be able to suggest relevant reasons for any variances identified. Reasons include:

3.2 Investigation of variances

To be able to control aspects of the business, management will need to investigate why the variances have happen. To decide which variances to investigate management will consider:

- The size of the variance – is it significant compared to the cost incurred

- The cost of investigating the variance – will it cost less to investigate and put it right than the variance itself

- Whether it is adverse or favourable – some companies will only investigate the adverse variances

- Ability to correct the variance – is the variance controllable in house (hours worked by staff) or uncontrollable (price charged by suppliers)

3.3 Causes of variances

Differences between actual values and budgeted values can occur for a number of reasons.

One of the main reasons is that when producing a budget we are trying to predict the future. Prediction of the future is not an exact science and is it is therefore extremely difficult to get it 100% correct.

This leads to the budgeted figures not being as accurate as they could be and therefore actual values are different from these.

3.4 Materials

Quality of materials used. If production uses a **higher quality** material then it will **cost more** to purchase. If a **lower quality** material is used it will be **cheaper** to purchase.

Quantity of materials used. If **more material** is required than planned for then this will **increase the cost**. If **less material** is required then this should **reduce the cost**.

Combination of quality and quantity. Higher quality costs more but may well lead to less wastage so use less. Lower quality costs less but may lead to more wastage so use more.

3.5 Labour

Grade of labour used. If a **higher grade** of labour is used then they will require **higher remuneration**. If a **lower grade** of labour is used then they will require as **lower remuneration**

Time taken to produce output. If the actual time taken is **longer** than budgeted then this will **cost more** but if actual time taken is **shorter** than budgeted then it will **cost less**.

Overtime. If there is extra time needed to complete the production then this may have to lead to having to pay some staff overtime. This is often paid at a **higher rate** than normal hours. This will **increase** the labour costs.

3.5 Overheads

If overheads are **absorbed based on labour hours** worked the same causes issues mentioned above can have an impact on the actual cost i.e. if there is an **under or over estimate of the hours** required in the budget this will impact on the overhead cost.

There could also be an variance due to the budgeted **cost** of the overheads, the actual could be higher or lower than planned.

3.6 Possible solutions for variances

There are a number of possible solutions for variances that arise:

- A change of supplier may be an option for improving prices for materials.

- Updating machinery may make the usage of materials better and may also reduce the number of hours the labour force work for.

- Better quality control over the materials that are used in production may reduce wastage.

- Better supervision of staff may reduce idle time and errors in production.

- Increased training may reduce errors and make the staff more efficient.

- Closer monitoring of budgets may make the budgets more accurate.

This list is not exhaustive and it would be necessary to take each variance in turn and investigate the best way to improve the situation.

4 Summary

This chapter has demonstrated how **cost behaviours** are used to predict costs at activity levels different to budget and to produce **flexed** budgets. It will be necessary to be able to identify cost behaviours and use them to produce a flexed budget to then compare with actual results or **calculate variances**.

Another important aspect of this chapter is **analysis of variances** including possible causes and solutions to these variances

Test your knowledge

Having completed Chapter 9 you should now be able to attempt:

Practice Activities 35 and 36

Answers to chapter activities

Activity 1

Batches sold and produced	1,000	1,500	2,000
Sale Revenue	40,000	60,000	80,000
Variable cost			
Direct Materials	4,000	6,000	8,000
Direct Labour	3,800	5,700	7,600
Overheads	7,200	10,800	14,400
Semi-variable costs	4,500		
Variable element		3,000	4,000
Fixed element		2,500	2,500
Fixed cost	3,500	3,500	3,500
Total cost	23,000	31,500	40,000
Total profit	17,000	28,500	40,000
Profit per batch (to 2 decimal places)	17.00	19.00	20.00

KAPLAN PUBLISHING

Activity 2

	Flexed Budget	Actual	Variance value	Favourable or Adverse
Volume Sold	1,400	1,400		
	£	£	£	
Sale Revenue	56,000	60,000	4,000	F
Less costs:				
Direct Materials	5,600	6,000	400	A
Direct Labour	5,320	5,300	20	F
Overheads	10,080	10,100	20	A
Semi-variable costs	FC = 2,500 VC = 2,800 Total = 5,300	5,500	200	A
Fixed cost	3,500	3,500	0	0
Operating profit	26,200	29,600	3,400	F

Short term decision making

Introduction

There are a number of calculations that can be completed to aid decision making in the short term. Within this chapter we will consider a number of different techniques that are required in different situations.

KNOWLEDGE
Identify costs and the correct classification - fixed, variable, semi-variable and stepped (2.2)
Explain the effect of changing activity levels on unit costs (3.1)
Identify the considerations affecting short-term decision making using – relevant costs, break-even analysis, margin of safety, target profit, profit-volume analysis and limiting factors (3.3)

SKILLS
Prepare estimates of future income and costs for decision making (3.4)
Prepare reports in an appropriate format and present these to management within the required timescales (3.5)

CONTENTS
1 Relevant costing
2 Cost-volume-profit (CVP) analysis
3 CVP charts
4 Limiting factors

1 Relevant costing

1.1 The concept of relevant costing

Any form of decision-making process involves making a choice between two or more alternatives. Decisions will generally be based on taking the route that maximises shareholder value, so all decisions will be taken using relevant costs and revenues.

1.2 Relevant costs and revenues

Relevant costs and revenues are those costs and revenues that change as a direct result of a decision that is taken. When looking at appraising an investment you should only consider the following to be relevant:

- **Future costs and revenues** – costs and revenues that occur once the investment has been made

- **Cash flows rather than profits** – profits can be manipulated by accounting concepts like depreciation. Cash flows are more accurate

- **Incremental costs and revenues** – any extra cost or revenue generated by an investment that would not arise otherwise e.g. an extra amount of fixed costs due only to the investment decision

- **Opportunity costs** – the best alternative that is forgone in taking a decision i.e. if the workforce had to be moved from one project to another the company would miss out on the contribution the workforce should have been producing.

- **Avoidable costs** – any cost that would only occur as a result of taking the decision. If the investment did not go ahead then the cost would not be incurred.

- **Variable costs** – as activity increases the total variable cost incurred increases. There is a direct relationship between production activity and variable costs. Unless told otherwise variable costs and the variable element of the semi-variable costs are relevant to a decision.

1.3 Non relevant costs

Costs that can be ruled out when making a decision come under the following categories:

- **Sunk costs** – past or historic costs that cannot be changed i.e. any research and development that has already been carried out will not be used in the decision.

- **Committed costs** – cost that cannot be avoided and will be incurred whether or not the project is done.

- **Non cash flow costs** – depreciation and net book values are accounting concepts and are not relevant costs

- **Fixed costs** – tend to come under the umbrella of committed costs so are not relevant. Be careful though because if the fixed cost were to step up as a direct result of a decision taken then the extra would be relevant.

 Example

It is the beginning of 20X1 and a decision needs to be made about whether to use machine A or machine B. The following information is available:

	Machine A		Machine B	
	20X9	201X	20X9	201X
Variable cost per unit	£10	£8	£12	£10
Fixed cost in total	£900	£1000	£900	£1000

The relevant cost for Machine A is:

The relevant cost for Machine B is:

Solution

If we consider the 20X9 costs, both the fixed and the variable, we can reject these as they are last year costs and are sunk costs, therefore irrelevant costs.

If we consider the 201X costs, we can reject expected fixed costs since they are the same ($7,000) for both machines and can therefore be ignored.

The only relevant costs in this situation are the future variable costs.

The relevant cost for Machine A is £8

The relevant cost for Machine B is £10

Machine A is the cheapest therefore the decision would be to use Machine A.

With regards **short term** decision making we assume that **fixed costs** are **non-relevant** cost so we can approach decisions using the **marginal costing technique.**

2 Cost-volume-profit (CVP) analysis

2.1 Introduction

Short term decisions could include:

*   how many units do we need to sell to make a certain profit?

*   how many units do we need to sell to cover our costs?

*   by how much will profit fall if price is lowered by £1?

*   what will happen to our profits if we rent an extra factory but find that we can operate at only half capacity?

The above questions can be answered by using cost-volume-profit (CVP) analysis.

2.2 Approach to CVP

CVP analysis makes a number of assumptions as follows.

*   Costs are assumed to be either **fixed** or **variable**, or at least **separable into these elements**.

*   Fixed costs remain fixed throughout the range charted.

*   Variable costs change in direct proportion to volume.

*   Economies or diseconomies of scale are ignored; this ensures that **the variable cost per unit is constant**.

*   Selling prices do not change with volume.

*   Efficiency and productivity do not change with volume.

*   It is applied to a single product or static mix of products.

*   We look at the effect a change in volume has on **contribution** (not profit). Therefore we use **marginal costing**.

*   Volume is the only factor affecting cost.

*   Contribution per unit = selling price per unit – total variable cost per unit.

*   Linearity is appropriate.

While some of the assumptions may seem unrealistic, over the short term considered, they are often a **reasonable approximation** to the true position.

There are a number of calculations and formulas that make up CVP analysis:

- Breakeven point

- Margin of safety

- Target profit

- Profit/volume ratio

2.3 Breakeven point

The **breakeven point** is the volume of sales at which neither a profit nor a loss is made. When there is no profit or loss we can assume that total fixed costs equal total contribution

The breakeven point in units can then be found using the following formula.

$$\text{Breakeven point} = \frac{\text{Fixed cost}}{\text{Contribution/unit}}$$

 Example

Breakeven point

Rachel's product, the 'Steadyarm', sells for £50. It has a variable cost of £30 per unit. Rachel's total fixed costs are £40,000 per annum.

What is her breakeven point?

Solution

To break even we want just enough contribution to cover the total fixed costs of £40,000.

We therefore want total contribution of £40,000.

Each unit of sales gives contribution of 50 − 30 = £20.

Therefore the breakeven point in units

$$= \frac{\text{Total fixed costs}}{\text{Contribution per unit}} = \frac{£40,000}{£20} = 2,000 \text{ units}$$

We can show that this calculation is correct as below.

	£
Total contribution (2,000 units × £20)	40,000
Total fixed costs	(40,000)
Profit/loss	0

Breakeven point can also be expressed in sales revenue terms. We know we have to sell 2,000 units to breakeven and we know the selling price is £50. The breakeven point in sales revenue is therefore £100,000.

2.4 Margin of safety

The margin of safety is the amount by which the anticipated (budgeted) sales can fall before the business makes a loss. It can be expressed in absolute units or relative percentage terms.

Margin of safety (units) = Budgeted sales units – Breakeven sales units

$$\text{Margin of safety (\%)} = \frac{\text{Budgeted sales units - Breakeven sales units}}{\text{Budgeted sales unit}} \times 100$$

 Example

Margin of Safety

Rachel's product, the 'Steadyarm', sells for £50. It has a variable cost of £30 per unit. Rachel's total fixed costs are £40,000 per annum. Rachel is expecting to achieve sales of 3,600 units.

What is her margin of safety?

Solution

To calculate the margin of safety we first need to know the breakeven point in units. From the previous example we know that for Rachel to breakeven she needs to sell 2,000 units.

$$= \frac{\text{Total fixed costs}}{\text{Contribution per unit}} = \frac{£40,000}{£20} = 2,000 \text{ units}$$

We can then work out the margin of safety in units:

= Budgeted sales units – Breakeven sales units

= 3,600 – 2,000 = 1,600 units

And then the margin of safety as a percentage of budgeted sales units

$$= \frac{\text{Budgeted sales units - Breakeven sales units}}{\text{Budgeted sales unit}} \times 100$$

$$= \frac{3,600 - 2,000}{3,600} \times 100 = 44.4\%$$

Margin of safety can also be expressed in sales revenue terms. In the example above we know we have a margin of safety of 1,600 units and the selling price for each of these units is £50. The sales revenue margin of safety is therefore £80,000.

 Activity 1

Camilla

Camilla makes a single product, the Wocket. During 201X she plans to make and sell 3,000 Wockets and has estimated the following:

	per unit
	£
Selling Price	15
Material	3
Labour	5
Variable overhead	2

Total fixed costs are budgeted to be £12,000

(a) Calculate the contribution per unit earned by each Wocket.

(b) Calculate Camilla's breakeven point in units.

(c) Calculate Camilla's breakeven point in revenue.

(d) Calculate Camilla's margin of safety in units

(e) Calculate Camilla's margin of safety in revenue

(f) Calculate Camilla's margin of safety as a percentage of budgeted sales

2.5 Achieving a target profit

A similar approach to breakeven analysis can be used to find the sales volume at which a particular profit is made. When calculating the breakeven point we wanted to find the number of units that would mean that contribution equalled fixed costs. Now if we know the required profit we can add this to the fixed costs to find the amount of contribution we need to cover both fixed costs and to generate the required profit.

Sales volume to achieve a particular profit

$$= \frac{\text{Total fixed costs} + \text{required profit}}{\text{Contribution/unit}}$$

Example

Achieving a target profit

Information as with Rachel above but we now want to know how many units must be sold to make a profit of £100,000.

To achieve a profit of £100,000, we require sufficient contribution firstly to cover the fixed costs (£40,000) and secondly, having covered fixed costs, we require sufficient contribution to give a profit of £100,000. Therefore our required contribution is £140,000.

Sales volume to achieve a profit of £100,000

$$= \frac{\text{Total fixed costs} + \text{required profit}}{\text{Contribution/unit}}$$

$$= \frac{£40,000 + £100,000}{£20}$$

$$= 7,000 \text{ units}$$

We can show that this is the case with a summarised profit and loss account.

	£
Sales (7,000 × £50)	350,000
Variable cost (7,000 × £30)	(210,000)
Total fixed costs	(40,000)
Profit	100,000

2.6 Profit/Volume ratio

The P/V ratio is a measure of the rate at which profit (or, strictly, contribution) is generated with sales volume, as measured by revenue. An alternative name which provides a more accurate description is the contribution/sales (C/S) ratio.

$$\text{P/V ratio} = \frac{\text{Contribution per unit}}{\text{Selling price}}$$

It tells us what **proportion of the selling price is contributing to our fixed overhead and profits.**

If, for example, the P/V ratio was 40% this would mean that 40% of the selling price was contribution which means therefore that the remaining 60% is variable cost.

It can be **used in the breakeven point and the target profit** calculations to be able to calculate the **answer in terms of sales value** (rather than volume).

Breakeven point in sales value $= \dfrac{\text{Total fixed costs}}{\text{P/V ratio}}$

Sales value giving a profit £X $= \dfrac{\text{Total fixed costs} + \text{required profit}}{\text{P/V ratio}}$

When using the P/V ratio is calculations the **decimal format** is used rather than the percentage i.e. 0.4 rather than 40%

 Example

P/V ratio

We return to the 'Steadyarm' example, where the product sells for £50, has a variable cost of £30 per unit and fixed costs and £40,000 per annum.

What value of sales will give a profit of £100,000?

Sales value giving profit £100,000 means that the required contribution is £140,000

$= \dfrac{\text{Total fixed costs} + \text{required profit}}{\text{P/V ratio}}$

$= \dfrac{£40,000 + £100,000}{0.4\ (W)}$

$= £350,000$

which corresponds with 7,000 units (as before) at £50 sales value per unit.

Working

P/V ratio $= \dfrac{\text{Contribution}}{\text{Selling price}} = \dfrac{£20}{£50} = 0.4$

Activity 2

Camilla

Camilla makes a single product, the Wocket. During 201X she plans to make and sell 3,000 Wockets and has estimated the following:

	per unit £
Selling Price	15
Material	3
Labour	5
Variable overhead	2

Total fixed costs are budgeted to be £12,000

Target profit £150,000

(a) Calculate the P/V ratio

(b) Calculate Camilla's breakeven point in revenue.

(c) Calculate the sales revenue that Camilla would require to meet her target profit.

3 CVP charts

3.1 Breakeven charts

We can show our analysis diagrammatically in a breakeven chart.

Breakeven chart showing fixed and variable cost lines

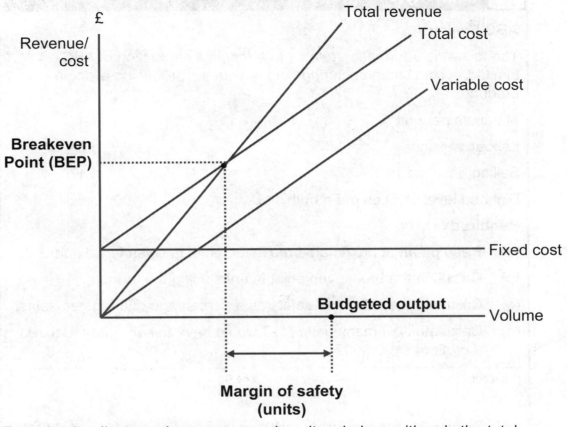

To make the diagram clearer we can show it as below, with only the total cost line on the graph.

Breakeven chart showing total cost line

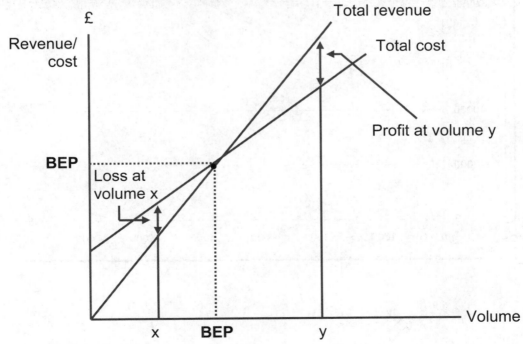

Activity 3

ABC Limited

The following information relates to a month's production of ABC Limited, a small manufacturing company mass producing a single product.

Materials per unit	£4
Labour per unit	£6
Selling price per unit	£17
Planned level of sales per month	7,000 units

Required

(a) Read off an approximate breakeven point in sales value and units.

(b) Calculate the breakeven point in units using the formula.

(c) Calculate the margin of safety as a percentage of budgeted sales.

(d) Calculate how many units ABC would have to sell if they required a profit of £100,000?

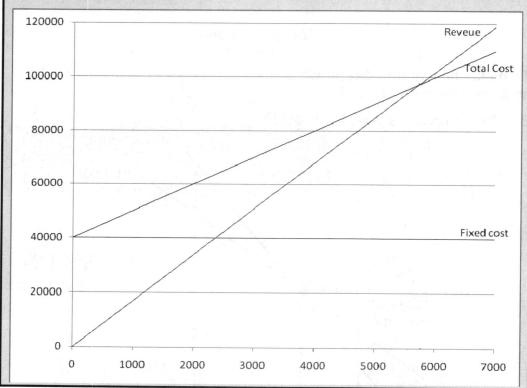

3.2 Profit-volume (P/V) chart

A P/V chart is another way of presenting the information.

P/V chart

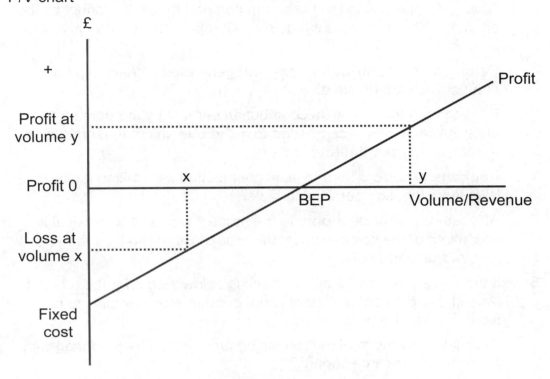

Note that at a **sales volume of nil**, the **total loss** will be the same as the business's **fixed costs**.

4 Limiting factors

4.1 Introduction

If a company makes more than one product it may be necessary to amend the production due to a lack of one the following resources – material, labour, machine time or cash. To do this they can use a procedure called Limiting factor analysis or Key factor analysis.

Limiting factor analysis can only be used if only one of the resources is limited. If there are two or more resources in restricted supply, we would use the technique of linear programming, which is not in this syllabus.

4.2 Approach to limiting factor analysis

There is a step by step process to completing limiting factor analysis

1 **Determine the resource that is in scarce supply** (the limiting factor), by multiplying the maximum demand for each product by the amount of the resources it requires. Compare this to what is available.

2 **Calculate the contribution per unit** generated by each type of product we want to make.

3 For each product divide its contribution per unit by the number of units of scarce resource needed to make one unit of that product (**contribution per limiting factor**).

4 **Rank the products** from highest contribution per limiting factor to lowest contribution per limiting factor.

5 **Allocate the scarce supply** to the product ranked 1 and calculate how much of the scarce supply this would use to produce the required demand.

6 If there is any scarce supply remaining follow step 5 for the product ranked 2 and so on until there is not enough scarce supply to match the demand for a product.

7 Calculate how much of the remaining product can be produced with the remaining scarce supply.

8 Calculate the total contribution from the new production plan and the overall profit.

 Example

Truffle Ltd

Truffle Ltd makes 3 products the Dog, the Hound and the Canine. The money to pay for the resources needed for next month's production are as follows:

Material £10,000

Labour £10,000

Variable Overheads £15,000

Below are the details for a unit each product:

	Dog £	Hound £	Canine £
Selling price	10	12	15
Material cost	2	3	2

Labour cost	1	3	4
Other variable costs	2	4	4
Maximum monthly demand	1,000	1,500	1,250

Total fixed costs £9,000

What is Truffle's optimal production plan for the next month?

Solution

Step 1 – identify the limiting factor

To be able to meet the maximum demand for all the products the requirements would be as follows:

Material = (2 × 1000) + (3 × 1500) + (2 × 1250) = £9,000

Labour = (1 × 1000) + (3 × 1500) + (4 × 1250) = £10,500

Other variable costs = (2 × 1000) + (4 × 1500) + (4 × 1250) = £13,000

Therefore the labour cost is the limiting factor as there is enough cash available to cover the cost of materials and other variable costs.

Step 2 - calculate the contribution per unit

	Dog £	Hound £	Canine £
Selling price	10	12	15
Material cost	(2)	(3)	(2)
Labour cost	(1)	(3)	(4)
Other variable costs	(2)	(4)	(4)
Contribution per unit	5	2	5

Step 3 – calculate the contribution per limiting factor

	Dog £	Hound £	Canine £
Contribution per unit	5	2	5
Limiting factor per unit	1	3	4
Contribution per limiting factor	5	0.66	1.25

Step 4 - rank the products

	Dog £	Hound £	Canine £
Contribution per limiting factor	5	0.66	1.25
Rank	1	3	2

Steps 5 to 8 - allocate the scarce supply

Product in rank order	Units	LF per unit £	Total LF £	Contribution £
Dog	1,000	1	1,000	5,000
Canine	1,250	4	5,000	6,250
Hound	1,333 (W)	3	4,000β	2,666

LF available	£10,000
Total contribution	13,916
Less fixed costs	(9,000)
Profit	4,916

Working

There is only £4000 left to spend on labour once maximum demand is allocated to the other products (β = balancing amount). This means that Truffle will be able to make 1333 complete Hounds (4000/3 = 1333.33).

Activity 4

ABC

ABC makes three products with the following estimated costs and revenues.

	A	B	C
Selling price (£)	20	25	30
Variable cost per unit (£)	10	11	14
Amount of material X used per unit (kg)	2	2	4
Maximum demand (units)	250	100	200

Total fixed costs £12,500

Due to a shortage in the market, only 800 kg are available.

Required

Using limiting factor analysis complete the table below to determine the production plan that will optimise profit.

	A	B	C
Selling price (£)			
Variable cost per unit (£)			

Contribution per unit (£)			
LF per unit (kg)			
Contribution per LF (£)			
Rank			

Production Plan

Product in rank order	Units	LF per unit (kg)	Total LF (kg)	Contribution (£)
1				
2				
3				
		Total LF	800kg	
			Total Contribution	
			Fixed costs	
			Profit	

Activity 5

Dunnsports

Dunnsports make a variety of sports goods. One of its product groups is cricket boots and they make a range of five styles. You are given the following data for the forthcoming quarter.

	Gower	Boycott	Willis	Taylor	Miller
Selling price	£27.50	£30.00	£28.50	£29.00	£25.00
Variable costs per unit:					
Direct material	£8.00	£8.50	£8.25	£8.50	£7.75
Direct labour at £7.50 per hour	£9.00	£9.75	£8.25	£9.38	£7.50
Forecast sales/production	500	510	520	500	510

Shortly after the budgeted output was agreed a machine breakdown occurred and, as parts are not available immediately, labour hours will be limited to 2,675 hours.

Required

Complete the table below to calculate the production schedule that will optimise profit, assuming that the actual sales per product will not exceed the forecast figures quoted.

	Gower	Boycott	Willis	Taylor	Miller
Selling price (£)					
Variable cost per unit (£)					
Contribution per unit (£)					
LF per unit (hours)					
Contribution per LF (£)					
Rank					

Product in rank order	Units	LF per unit (hours)	Total LF (hours)	Contribution (£)
1				
2				
3				
4				
5				
		Total LF	2,675	
			Total Contribution	

5 Summary

In this chapter we have considered the approaches required to make short-term decisions about operating levels. CVP analysis recognises that changes in profit arise from changes in contribution which, in turn, is directly related to activity levels. Thus, we can use contribution per unit to calculate the required activity level to achieve a particular profit level, including zero (breakeven point). The formulas are not provided in the exam so make sure you have learnt them

Breakeven point in units

$$\frac{\text{Fixed cost}}{\text{Contribution/unit}}$$

Sales volume to achieve a particular profit

$$\frac{\text{Total fixed costs} + \text{required profit}}{\text{Contribution/unit}}$$

If we **know the beakeven point**, then we can also calculate the margin of safety

Margin of safety (units)

$$\text{Budgeted sales units} - \text{Breakeven sales units}$$

Margin of safety (%)

$$\frac{\text{Budgeted sales units} - \text{breakeven sales units}}{\text{Budgeted sales units}} \times 100\%$$

Using the Profit/Volume ratio the BEP and target profit calculation and produce values in sales revenue rather than units.

Profit/Volume ratio or **C/S** ratio

$$\frac{\text{Contribution per unit}}{\text{Selling price}}$$

Breakeven point in **sales revenue** terms (£)

$$\frac{\text{Fixed cost}}{\text{C/S ratio}}$$

Sales revenue (£) to achieve a particular profit

$$\frac{\text{Total fixed costs} + \text{required profit}}{\text{C/S ratio}}$$

Key factor analysis is a technique that we can use when we have a resource (materials, labour or machine time, for example) that is in short supply. Scarce resources should be allocated between products on the basis of the contribution that they earn per unit of scarce resource.

 Test your knowledge

Having completed Chapter 10 you should now be able to attempt:

Practice Activities 37, 38, 39, 40, 41 and 42

Answers to chapter activities

 Activity 1

(a) **Contribution per unit**

= Selling price per unit – Variable cost per unit

= £15 – £10 = **£5**

(b) **Breakeven point (units)**

= Total fixed costs / Contribution per unit

= £12,000/£5 = **2,400 units**

(c) **Breakeven point (revenue)**

= Breakeven point (units) × sales revenue per unit

= 2,400 units × £15 = **£36,000**

(d) **Margin of safety (units)**

= budgeted sales – breakeven point

= 3,000 – 2,400 = **600 units**

(e) **Margin of safety (revenue)**

= margin of safety (units) × sales revenue per unit

= 600 × £15 = **£9,000**

(a) **Margin of safety (%)**

= (budgeted sales – breakeven point)/budgeted sales × 100%

= (3,000 – 2,400)/3,000 × 100% = **20%**

 Activity 2

(a) **P/V ratio**

Contribution = 15 – (3+5+2) = 5
PV ratio = 15/5 = **0.3333333**

(b) **Breakeven point in revenue**

= £12,000/0.3333333 = **£36,000**

(c) **Sales revenue to meet the target profit.**

(£12,000 + £150,000)/0.3333333 = **£486000**

 Activity 3

(a) Breakeven point from graph

Approx £97,000 sales and 5,700 units.

(b) Breakeven point in units

$$\frac{\text{Fixed cost}}{\text{Contribution per unit}}$$

$$= \frac{£40,000}{£7}$$

= **5,715 units (rounding up)**

(c) Margin of safety (%)

$$\frac{\text{Budgeted sales units} - \text{Breakeven sales units}}{\text{Budgeted sales unit}} \times 100$$

$$= \frac{7,000 - 5715}{7,000} \times 100$$

=**18.36%**

(d) Target profit

$$\frac{\text{Total fixed costs} + \text{required profit}}{\text{Contribution/unit}}$$

$$= \frac{140,000}{7}$$

= **20,000 units**

Activity 4

ABC

	A	B	C
Selling price (£)	20	25	30
Variable cost per unit (£)	10	11	14
Contribution per unit	10	14	16
LF per unit (kg)	2	2	4
Contribution per LF (£)	5	7	4
Ranking	2	1	3

Production Plan

Product in rank order	Units	LF per unit (kg)	Total LF (kg)	Contribution (£)
1 B	100	2	200	14,000
2 A	250	2	500	2,500
3 C	25	4	100 β	400
		Total LF	800 kg	
			Total Contribution	16,900
			Fixed costs	(12,500)
			Profit	4,400

Activity 5

	Gower	Boycott	Willis	Taylor	Miller
Selling price (£)	27.50	30	28.50	29	25
Variable cost per unit (£)	17	18.25	16.50	17.88	15.25
Contribution per unit (£)	10.50	11.75	12	11.12	9.75
LF per unit (hours) (W)	1.2	1.3	1.1	1.25	1.0
Contribution per LF (£)	8.75	9.04	10.91	8.9	9.75
Rank	5	3	1	4	2

Product in rank order	Units	LF per unit (hours)	Total LF (hours)	Contribution (£)
1 Willis	520	1.1	572	6,240
2 Miller	510	1.0	510	4,972.50
3 Boycott	510	1.3	663	5,992.50
4 Taylor	500	1.25	625	5,560
5 Gower	254	1.2	305 β	2,667
		Total LF	2,675	
		Total Contribution		25,432

Working – LF per unit

Labour charge per unit/Labour charge per hour

Gower £9.00/ £7.50 = 1.2 hours per unit

Long term decision making

Introduction

In the previous chapter we looked at how contribution can be used to make short-term decisions, such as which products to make when we have a shortage of resources (e.g. materials, labour).

In this chapter the focus is on long-term investment decisions – usually lasting more than one year. This could vary from the decision to build a new factory to whether or not to discontinue a product range.

The investment appraisal techniques that are discussed in this chapter are the payback period, net present value method and the internal rate of return.

KNOWLEDGE

Explain the principles of discounted cash flow (3.2)

Identify the considerations affecting long-term decision making using payback and discounted cash flow methods (3.4)

SKILLS

Prepare estimates of future income and costs for decision making (3.4)

Prepare reports in an appropriate format and present these to management within the required timescales (3.5)

CONTENTS

1 Long-term investments
2 Predicting future cash flows
3 Payback period
4 Net present value and internal rate of return

1 Long-term investments

1.1 Introduction

The key characteristic of a capital investment project is the tying up of capital for a number of years, or for the long term, in order to earn profits or returns over the period.

1.2 What will the capital be invested in?

The most common investment you will encounter will be in **tangible fixed assets**, such as a new machine, factory or premises from which to operate a new service business.

Other less tangible forms of investment include **research and development**, **patent rights or goodwill** obtained on the purchase of an existing business.

1.3 What form will the returns take?

The purchase of a new fixed asset will often be with the intention of starting a new line of business – say the manufacturing of a new product, or the provision of a new or extended service. The returns will be the **net income** generated by the new business.

Alternatively, the investment may be to benefit the existing operations, such that **sales are increased** (where existing products/services are improved technologically or in quality) or **costs are reduced** (where production processes are updated or personnel reorganised). The returns will be measured as the **increase in net income or net reduction in costs** resulting from the investment.

1.4 Authorisation for a capital project

For projects involving a significant amount of capital investment, **authorisation** for its go-ahead will usually be given by the main board, or a sub-committee formed from the board for this purpose. Smaller projects (such as the replacement of an existing machine) may be within the authorisation limits of the manager of the area of business involved.

The decision will be based upon a **project proposal** using methods such as payback or net present value (discussed below).

KAPLAN PUBLISHING

1.5 Importance of non-financial factors

Although these appraisal methods will usually give a basis for a **recommendation as to whether or not the project should be accepted,** they will only be able to take account of monetary costs and benefits. **Qualitative factors** will also need to be considered when reaching a final decision – such as possible effects on staff morale (for example, if the project involves increased automation or considerable overtime), the environment, customer satisfaction and the business's status/reputation.

2   Predicting future cash flows

2.1 Introduction

Any potential investment will need to be evaluated with regards the costs and revenues that will occur i.e. the cashflow received from the investment activity. This will involve estimating sales, costs, capital expenditure, disposal proceeds and so on.

2.2 The cash flows under consideration

When estimating future cash flows we want to identify what difference the project will make therefore we only consider **future incremental** cash flows are relevant, e.g. the factory rent may be unaffected by the proposed project and would not be included when assessing the investment, whereas the purchase of a new machine is required so would be included.

As well as knowing what the future cash flows will be, we also need to know when they will occur. The time the investment starts we call time 0 or t = 0. Subsequent future cash flows are assumed to happen at year-ends, e.g. all of the sales and costs for the first year are assumed to be paid at the end of the first year this is called time 1 or t = 1.

If we do this for all the future cash flows of the project, then we will typically end up with a table like the following:

	t = 0 £000	Year 1 (t = 1) £000	Year 2 (t = 2) £000	Year 3 (t = 3) £000	Year 4 (t = 4) £000	Year 5 (t = 5) £000
Initial Investment	(100)					
Scrap value						30
Sales		40	50	60	50	40
Variable costs		(10)	(12)	(15)	(13)	(11)
Net cash flow	(100)	30	38	45	37	59

3 Payback period

3.1 Calculation

One way of assessing the viability of an investment is to calculate a payback period. This calculates how long it will take before the cost of initial investment is recovered.

If the annual cash flows are constant, then the calculation is very straightforward e.g. if I invest £100,000 and get cash back of £20,000 each year, then it will take 100/20 = 5 years to recover my investment.

However, if the annual cash flows vary, then we need to calculate the cumulative net position at the end of each year.

Using the example above:

Time	Cash flow £000	Cumulative position £000	Working to calculate the cumulative position
t = 0	(100)	(100)	
t = 1	30	(70)	(100) + 30
t = 2	38	(32)	(70) + 38
t = 3	45	13	(32) + 45
t = 4	37	50	13 + 37
t = 5	59	109	50 + 59

From this table we can see that we would recover the initial investment sometime in the third year as this is when the cumulative position initially becomes positive.

NB remember that t = 3 is the equivalent of 2 years and 12 months.

To be more accurate we need to examine the cash flows that occur during the third year in more detail. We assume that cashflows happen evenly through the year so there is an equal amount of sales revenue each month and an equal amount of costs each month, rather than all being paid at the year-end. This means that we will break even part way through the third year, rather than at the end of the year.

From the figures above we can see that £32,000 (*) is needed to break even during the third year. There is a total of £45,000 (**) in cash flow during that year. See extract of table below:

Time	Cash flow £000	Cumulative position £000
t = 2	38	**(32)***
t = 3	**45****	13

The payback period is therefore:

$= 2\frac{32}{45}$ or 2.71 years

0.71 of a year is 8 1/2 months

This could also be calculated as follows:

- Calculate the cash flow per month

  £45,000/12 = £3,750

- Calculate how many months are needed to cover remaining investment

  £32000/£3750 = 8.533 months

The payback period is then compared with the target payback that has been set, e.g. this company may have decided only to accept projects with paybacks lower than four years, in which case this project is acceptable.

Activity 1

A machine costs £100,000 now. We expect cash receipts of £30,000 in one year's time, £40,000 in two years' time, £60,000 in three years' time and £10,000 in four years' time.

Calculate the payback period for the investment by filling in the table below:

Time		Cash flow £000	Cumulative Cash flow £000
t = 0		(100)	
t = 1		30	
t = 2		40	
t = 3		60	
t = 4		10	

Payback is .... years and .... months

3.2 Advantages of payback period

(a) It is easy to calculate.

(b) It is easy to understand.

(c) It is **less affected by uncertainty** as the cash flows that are being considered are earlier forecasts.

(d) It can obviously be very useful in specific circumstances such as when the company has **liquidity problems** i.e. have cash available for a limited length of time, as it provides an estimate for how long cash will be tied up in the investment for.

3.3 Disadvantages of payback period

(a) **Flows outside the payback period are ignored**. If, for the same example as before, the cash flow in the fifth year had been £20,000 the payback period would be unaltered at 2 years 8 1/2 months.

(b) The **timing of flows within the payback period** is ignored. If, again for the same example, the first two years' receipts had been:

1st year   £50,000

2nd year   £18,000

again the payback period would be unaltered at 2 years 8 ½ months.

(c) It **ignores the time value of money** i.e. the interest that capital can earn. We shall see the relevance of this in the next sections on discounted cash flow.

(d) It does not provide a monetary value for the return available from the investment.

4 Net present value and Internal rate of return

4.1 The time value of money

A key concept in long-term decision-making is that money received today is worth more than the same sum received in the future, i.e. it has a **time value.**

Suppose you were offered £100 now or £100 in one year's time. Even though the sums are the same, most people would prefer the money now. The £100 in the future is effectively worth less to us than £100 now – the timing of the cash makes a difference.

The main reasons for this are as follows:

- **Investment opportunities**: the £100 received now could be deposited into a bank account and earn interest. It would therefore grow to become more than £100 in one year.

- **Inflation**: the £100 now will buy more goods than £100 in one year due to inflation.

- **Cost of capital**: the £100 received now could be used to reduce a loan or overdraft and save interest.

- **Risk**: the £100 now is more certain than the offer of money in the future.

To do calculations using the time value of money it needs to be expressed as an interest rate (often known as a cost of capital, a required return or a **discount rate**)

Suppose we felt that £100 now was worth the same to us as £110 offered in one year's time due to the factors above. We could say that our time value of money was estimated at 10% per annum.

Therefore £100 now is worth the same as £110 offered in one year. Alternatively we say that the £110 in one year has a present value of £100 now. This process of taking future cash flows and converting them into their equivalent present value now is called **discounting**.

To calculate the present value of any future cash flow we multiply the cash flow by a suitable discount factor (or present value factor):

Present value = future cash flow × discount factor

Discount factors are provided in assessment so you do not need to be able to calculate them but you will need to know how to use them.

For example, with a 10% discount rate, the discount factor for a cash flow at t=1 is 0.909. Thus the offer of receiving £110 in one year's time is worth in today's terms

Present value = 110 × 0.909 = £99.99

4.2   Net Present Value (NPV)

The use of the discount rate enables more accurate prediction of the return an investment will give. Future incremental cash flows can be discounted to present values and the values can then netted off against the initial investment to see what the overall return from the investment will be. This investment appraisal method is known as the **Net Present Value (NPV).**

There is a step by step procedure for completing an NPV calculation:

Step 1   Calculate the future incremental cash flows.

Step 2   Discount the cash flows so they are in today's terms (present values).

Step 3   Now the present values can be added up and netted off to give a net present value or NPV.

Step 4   If the NPV is positive, then it means that the cash inflows are worth more than the outflows and the project should be accepted.

Using the previous example with a discount rate of 10%, this could be set out as follows:

	t = 0 £000	Year 1 (t = 1) £000	Year 2 (t = 2) £000	Year 3 (t = 3) £000	Year 4 (t = 4) £000	Year 5 (t = 5) £000
Net cash flow	(100)	30	38	45	37	59
Discount factor	1	0.909	0.826	0.751	0.683	0.621
Present value	(100)	27.3	31.4	33.8	25.3	36.6

Net Present Value = (100) + 27.3 + 31.4 + 33.8 +25.3 + 36.6 = 54.4

The NPV = £54,400 positive, so the project should be undertaken.

Activity 2

A machine costs £80,000 to buy now. The predicted sales revenue and operating costs for the following 4 years are as follows:

Year	Sales Revenue £	Operating Cost £
1	40,000	20,000
2	70,000	20,000
3	80,000	40,000
4	90,000	80,000

The rate of interest applicable is 15%. Should we accept or reject the machine?

The relevant present value factors are:

	Year 1	Year 2	Year 3	Year 4
15%	0.870	0.756	0.658	0.572

	Year 0	Year 1	Year 2	Year 3	Year 4
Capital expenditure					
Sales income					
Operating costs					
Net cash flow					
PV Factor	1.000	0.870	0.756	0.658	0.572
Discounted cash flow					
Net present value					

The net present value is *positive/negative**
*delete as appropriate

Activity 3

Machine A costs £100,000, payable immediately. Machine B costs £120,000, half payable immediately and half payable in one year's time.

The net cash flows expected are as follows.

	A £	B £
at the end of 1 year	20,000	–
at the end of 2 years	60,000	60,000
at the end of 3 years	40,000	60,000
at the end of 4 years	30,000	80,000
at the end of 5 years	20,000	–

With interest at 5%, which machine should be selected?

The relevant present value factors are:

	Year 1	Year 2	Year 3	Year 4	Year 5
5%	0.952	0.907	0.864	0.823	0.784

Machine A

	Year 0	Year 1	Year 2	Year 3	Year 4	Year 5
Capital expenditure						
Net cash flow						
PV Factor	1.000	0.952	0.907	0.864	0.823	0.784
Discounted cash flow						
Net present value						

The net present value of machine A is *positive/negative**

*delete as appropriate

Machine B

	Year 0	Year 1	Year 2	Year 3	Year 4	Year 5
Capital expenditure						
Net cash flow						
PV Factor	1.000	0.952	0.907	0.864	0.823	0.784
Discounted cash flow						
Net present value						

The net present value of machine B is *positive/negative**
*delete as appropriate

Machine *A/B** should be selected as it has the *higher/lower** NPV
*delete as appropriate

4.3 Net Present Value of costs only

In some cases you may be asked to look at the operating costs of an investment only rather than the costs and revenues associated with the investment. In this case the step by step procedure is exactly the same but you will need to decide which investment is cheapest to run.

 Activity 4

Machine A costs £100,000, payable immediately. Machine B costs £80,000, payable immediately. The running costs expected are as follows.

	A £	B £
at the end of 1 year	20,000	20,000
at the end of 2 years	50,000	30,000
at the end of 3 years	30,000	40,000
at the end of 4 years	20,000	50,000
at the end of 5 years	10,000	60,000

With interest at 8%, which machine should be selected?

The relevant present value factors are:

	Year 1	Year 2	Year 3	Year 4	Year 5
8%	0.926	0.857	0.794	0.735	0.681

Machine A

	Year 0	Year 1	Year 2	Year 3	Year 4	Year 5
Capital expenditure						
Net cash flow						
PV Factor	1.000	0.926	0.857	0.794	0.735	0.681
Discounted cash flow						
Net present cost						

Machine B

	Year 0	Year 1	Year 2	Year 3	Year 4	Year 5
Capital expenditure						
Net cash flow						
PV Factor	1.000	0.926	0.857	0.794	0.735	0.681
Discounted cash flow						
Net present cost						

Machine *A/B** should be selected as it has the *higher/lower** NPC
*delete as appropriate

4.4   Advantages of NPV

(a)   It considers the **time value of money**.

(b)   It uses cash flows which are less subjective than profits. Profit measures rely on such things as depreciation and other policies which are to a certain extent subjective.

(c)   It considers the **whole life** of the project.

(d)   It provides a monetary value for the return from an investment.

KAPLAN PUBLISHING

4.5 Disadvantages of NPV

(a) Cash flows are future prediction and we are **unable to predict** the future with accuracy.

(b) Discounted cash flow as a concept is **more difficult** for a non-financial manager to understand.

(c) It may be difficult to **decide on which discount rate** to use when appraising a project.

4.6 The internal rate of return (IRR)

NPV calculates the monetray return an investment could provide at a given interest rate by discounting cash flows at a given cost of capital. The **IRR** calculates the **rate of return** (or discount rate) that the project is expected to achieve if it **breaks even** i.e. no profit or loss is made. The IRR is therefore the point where the **NPV of an investment is zero**.

For an investment, a graph of NPV against discount rate looks like the following:

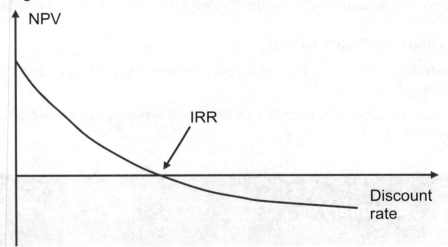

As the discount rate gets higher, the NPV gets smaller and then becomes negative. The cash flows are being discounted by a higher percentage therefore the present value of the cash flows becomes less.

The internal rate of return (IRR) is the discount rate that will cause the cash flow of a project to have a net present value equal to zero.

To decide on whether to invest using the IRR you need to compare the IRR with the discount rate that the company would like to use. If the chosen discount rate was somewhere between 10% and 15%, and the IRR of a project was 22% then we can still accept the project as our rate is less than the IRR, giving a positive NPV.

You will not have to calculate IRRs but you may need to be able to appraise a project based on the IRR.

Activity 5

If the company's cost of capital is 16% and the IRR is 14% the investment should go ahead.

True or false?

4.7 Advantages of IRR

(a) It considers the **time value of money**.

(b) It uses cash flows which are less subjective than profits. Profit measures rely on such things as depreciation and other policies which are to a certain extent subjective.

(c) It considers the **whole life** of the project.

(d) It provides a **percentage return** that is easier for non-financial managers to understand.

(e) It can be calculated without deciding on the desired cost of capital

4.8 Disadvantages of IRR

(a) Cash flows are future prediction and we are **unable to predict** the future with accuracy.

(b) It does not provide a monetary value for the return available from the investment.

5 Summary

In this chapter we have considered the mechanics, the advantages and the disadvantages of various investment appraisal techniques. In the context of an examination, you must be able to **calculate** the **payback period and the Net Present Value of a project.**

The payback period calculates how long it will take to recover the initial investment in a project. The Net Present Value, on the other hand, is an appraisal technique that takes the time value of money into account and calculates the return from an investment in monetary terms.

You do not need to be able to calculate the IRR of a project, but you do need to use it to make investment decisions. Since the IRR is the discount rate at which a project has a NPV equal to zero, a cost of capital (or discount rate) which is less than the IRR will give rise to a positive NPV (and is therefore considered to be an 'acceptable investment').

If there are conflicts between the NPV and payback investment appraisal methods then the NPV is the strongest measure so the **NPV result will over rule the payback.**

 Test your knowledge

Having completed Chapter 11 you should now be able to attempt:

Practice Activities 43, 44, 45, 46, 47, 48, 49, 50 and 51

Answers to chapter activities

Activity 1

Time	Cash flow £000	Cumulative position £000	Working £000
t = 0	(100)	(100)	
t = 1	30	(70)	(100) + 30
t = 2	40	(30)	(70) + 40
t = 3	60	30	(30) + 60
t = 4	10	40	30 + 10

Payback period is 2 years and 6 months

$= 2\,^{30}/_{60}$ or 2.5 years

Or

£60,000/12 = £5000

£30,000/£5000 = 6 months

Activity 2

A machine costs £80,000 now. We expect cash receipts of £20,000 in one year's time, £50,000 in two years' time, £40,000 in three years' time and £10,000 in four years' time. The rate of interest applicable is 15%. Should we accept or reject the machine?

The relevant present value factors are:

	Year 1	Year 2	Year 3	Year 4
15%	0.870	0.756	0.658	0.572

	Year 0	Year 1	Year 2	Year 3	Year 4
Capital expenditure	(80,000)				
Sales revenue		40,000	70,000	80,000	90,000
Operating costs		(20,000)	(20,000)	(40,000)	(80,000)
Net cash flow		20,000	50,000	40,000	10,000
PV Factor	1.000	0.870	0.756	0.658	0.572
Discounted cash flow	(80,000)	17,400	37,800	26,320	5,720
Net present value	7,240				

The net present value is *positive*.

 Activity 3

Machine A

	Year 0	Year 1	Year 2	Year 3	Year 4	Year 5
Capital expenditure	(100,000)					
Net cash flow		20,000	60,000	40,000	30,000	20,000
PV Factor	1.000	0.952	0.907	0.864	0.823	0.784
Discounted cash flow	(100,000)	19,040	54,420	34,560	24,690	15,680
Net present value	48,390					

The net present value of machine A is *positive*.

Machine B

	Year 0	Year 1	Year 2	Year 3	Year 4	Year 5
Capital expenditure	(60,000)	(60,000)				
Net cash flow			60,000	60,000	80,000	0
PV Factor	1.000	0.952	0.907	0.864	0.823	0.784
Discounted cash flow	(60,000)	(57,120)	54,420	51,840	65,840	0
Net present value	54,980					

The net present value of machine B is *positive*

Machine B has the higher NPV therefore the return from using this machine is better than machine A. Machine B should be selected.

 Activity 4

Machine A costs £100,000, payable immediately. Machine B costs £80,000, payable immediately. The running costs expected are as follows.

	A	B
	£	£
at the end of 1 year	20,000	20,000
at the end of 2 years	50,000	30,000
at the end of 3 years	30,000	40,000
at the end of 4 years	20,000	50,000
at the end of 5 years	10,000	60,000

With interest at 8%, which machine should be selected?

The relevant present value factors are:

	Year 1	Year 2	Year 3	Year 4	Year 5
8%	0.926	0.857	0.794	0.735	0.681

KAPLAN PUBLISHING

Machine A

	Year 0	Year 1	Year 2	Year 3	Year 4	Year 5
Capital expenditure	100,000					
Net cash flow		20,000	50,000	30,000	20,000	10,000
PV Factor	1.000	0.926	0.857	0.794	0.735	0.681
Discounted cash flow	100,000	18,520	42,850	23,820	14,700	6,810
Net present cost	209,700					

Machine B

	Year 0	Year 1	Year 2	Year 3	Year 4	Year 5
Capital expenditure	80,000					
Net cash flow		20,000	30,000	40,000	50,000	60,000
PV Factor	1.000	0.926	0.857	0.794	0.735	0.681
Discounted cash flow	80,000	18,520	25,710	31,760	36,750	40,860
Net present cost	233,600					

Machine *A* should be selected as it has the *lower* NPV of cost

 Activity 5

False. The IRR is lower than the cost of capital therefore the investment will have broken even at 14% and be a negative NPV at 16%.

QUESTIONS

Key techniques questions

1 Principles of cost accounting

Activity 1

A cost centre is defined as:

A   A unit of product or service for which costs are accumulated.

B   A production or service location, function, activity or item of equipment for which costs are accumulated.

C   Costs that relate directly to a unit

D   Costs that contain both a fixed and a variable element

Activity 2

Direct costs are:

A   A unit of product or service for which costs are accumulated.

B   A production or service location, function, activity or item of equipment for which costs are accumulated.

C   Costs that relate directly to a unit

D   Costs that contain both a fixed and a variable element

Activity 3

A semi-variable cost is:

A   A unit of product or service for which costs are accumulated.

B   A production or service location, function, activity or item of equipment for which costs are accumulated.

C   A cost that relate directly to a unit

D   A cost that contains both a fixed and a variable element

 Activity 4

The electricity used in a factory has a semi-variable cost behaviour. The manager wants to know how much electricity to budget for if he was to make 75 units.

Units	Total cost
10	120
50	200
100	300

The cost for the electricity for 75 units is:

A   £150

B   £100

C   £250

D   £137.50

KAPLAN PUBLISHING

Activity 5

Biscuit Making Company

The general manager has given you the task of supplying cost data for the manufacture of a specific brand of chocolate biscuit for 20X9 on the basis of projected costs. A cost clerk has given you data on variable and fixed costs, which is relevant over the range of production.

(a) **Complete the budgeted cost schedule for the different levels of production**

BUDGETED COST SCHEDULE		YEAR 20X9			
		ACTIVITY (Packets)			
		150,000	175,000	200,000	225,000
Description	£	£	£	£	
Variable costs					
Direct material	£12,000				
Direct labour	£9,000				
Packing costs	£1,500				
Fixed costs:					
Depreciation costs	£12,000				
Rent and rates	£26,000				
Supervisory costs	£12,000				
Administration costs	£8,000				
Total costs	£80,500				
Cost per packet (2 decimal places)	£0.54				

The cost per packet has *increased/decreased** because the fixed cost per unit has *increased/decreased**

*delete as appropriate

2 Material costs

 Activity 6

Match the document with the correct situation?

Goods received note	Form completed by the purchasing department to order supplies
Purchase order	Form completed by the stores department detailing stock requirements
Purchase requisition	Details the amount due to be paid and the date payment is due by
Stores record card	Form received with goods on delivery
Delivery note	Document completed to show the movement of stock
Purchase invoice	Document completed by stores on receipt of goods

Activity 7

Kiveton Cleaning Services supplies its employees with protective clothing. One such item is protective gloves.

Records from the stores department for January showed:

1 Jan	Opening stock
	150 pairs @ £2 each
7 Jan	Purchases
	40 pairs @ £1.90
15 Jan	Issues
	30 pairs
29 Jan	Issues
	35 pairs

Calculate the value of the issues and the closing stock if the FIFO method is used to price the usage

KAPLAN PUBLISHING

Stores Record Card FIFO

Material:　　　Protective gloves

Code:　　　　1607

Date	Details	Receipts		Issues			Stock		
		Pairs	£	Pairs	Price	£	Pairs	Price	£

What is the double entry for the receipt on the 7th January?

A　　Dr Bank, Cr Materials

B　　Dr Production, Cr Materials

C　　Dr Materials, Cr Bank

D　　Dr Materials, Cr Production

Activity 8

Cavernelli runs a pizza house.

The stock and usage of pizza bases for December was:

		Units	Value £
Opening stock	1 Dec	200	180
Purchases	3 Dec	800	800
Purchases	20 Dec	1,200	1,140
Usage	w/e 7 Dec	400	
	w/e 14 Dec	350	
	w/e 21 Dec	410	
	w/e 28 Dec	475	

Calculate the value of issues and the closing stock using the FIFO method of pricing (show figures to the nearest £).

The issues are priced at the end of each week.

Stores Record Card FIFO

Material: Pizza

Code: 1626

Date	Details	Receipts		Issues			Stock		
		Units	£	Units	Price	£	Units	Price	£

Activity 9

Crescent Engineering use a standard component AB3 and the stock, receipts and issues for the month of September were:

Opening stock 75 units @ £40 = £3,000.

Date	Receipts (units)	Unit cost £	Issues to production (units)
1 Sept	100	40	
10 Sept	75	42	
15 Sept			60
20 Sept			55
23 Sept	45	42	
30 Sept			50

The company uses the weighted average cost method for pricing issues and valuing stock.

Calculate the value of the usage for the month and the value of closing stock (figures to the nearest £1).

Stores Record Card AVCO

Material: Component AB3

Code: 010203

Date	Details	Receipts		Issues			Stock		
		Units	£	Units	Price	£	Units	Price	£

Activity 10

Retail Store Company

Issues are costed from the warehouse and transport department using the weighted average method.

Complete the stores ledger card below for an item of stock in the clothing department for the month of May 20X8 using the weighted average method for costing issues and valuing stock.

Note: Figures in the total columns should be shown to the nearest £. The company's policy is to round prices per unit to three decimal places.

Stores Record Card

Department: Month:

Date	Receipts			Issues			Balance		
	Quantity	Price £	Total £	Quantity	Price £	Total £	Quantity	Price £	Total £
1/5 Balance							2,420	5.200	12,584
7/5	2,950	5.500	16,226						
11/5	3,200	5.700	18,239						
14/5				4,105					
21/5	1,535	5.400	8,289						
27/5				1,800					
30/5				2,600					

What is the double entry for the issue on the 27th May?

A   Dr Bank, Cr Materials

B   Dr Materials, Cr Bank

C   Dr Materials, Cr Production

D   Dr Production, Cr Materials

Activity 11

Navneet Ltd

Identify the method of stock valuation and complete the stock record card shown below for steel component Magic, for the month of May 20Y0.

Note: Figures in the total columns should be shown to the nearest £. The company's policy is to round prices per unit to two decimal places.

STOCK RECORD CARD FOR STEEL COMPONENT MAGIC								
	Receipts			Issues			Balance	
Date 20Y0	Quantity kg	Cost per kg (£)	Total cost (£)	Quantity kg	Cost per kg (£)	Total cost (£)	Quantity kg	£
Balance as at 1 May							25,000	50,000
9 May	30,000	2.30	69,000				55,000	119,000
12 May				40,000		84,500		
18 May	20,000	2.50	50,000					
27 May				10,000				

The issue of component Magic on 12 May was for the production of product Abra, whilst that on the 27 May was for the production of product Cadabra.

The following cost accounting codes are used:

Code	Description
306	Stocks of component Magic
401	Work-in-progress – Product Abra
402	Work-in-progress – Product Cadabra
500	Creditors Control

Complete the journal below to record separately the FOUR cost accounting entries in respect of the two receipts and two issues during the month of May 20Y0

Date 20Y0	Code	Dr £	Cr £
9 May			
9 May			
12 May			
12 May			
18 May			
18 May			
27 May			
27 May			

 Activity 12

Ravenscar Engineering uses a standard component XZ7.

It estimates the following information regarding this unit:

Maximum weekly usage	600 units
Minimum weekly usage	400 units
Average weekly usage	500 units
Delivery period maximum	6 weeks
minimum 4 weeks	
average 5 weeks	

The working year is 50 weeks

Ordering costs are £25 per order and it costs £5 per unit per year to store the component.

Calculate:

- Re-order level

KAPLAN PUBLISHING

- Economic order quantity

- Maximum stock level

- Minimum stock level

3 Labour costs

 Activity 13

Below is the weekly timesheet for Ekta Plasm (employee number EP0516), who is paid as follows:

- For a basic six-hour shift every day from Monday to Friday - basic pay.

- For any overtime in excess of the basic six hours, on any day from Monday to Friday - the extra hours are paid at time-and-a-third.

- For three contracted hours each Saturday morning - basic pay.

- For any hours in excess of three hours on Saturday - the extra hours are paid at double time.

- For any hours worked on Sunday - paid at double time

- Any overtime worked is due to general work pressures

Complete the columns headed Basic pay, Overtime premium and Total pay. Zero figures should be entered in cells where appropriate.

Employee's weekly timesheet for week ending 24 April

Name:		Ekta Plasm		Cost centre:		Sewing	
Employee number: EP0516				Basic Pay per hour: £9			

	Hours spent on:		Notes	Basic pay £	Overtime premium £	Total pay £
	Production	Indirect work				
Monday	6					
Tuesday	3	3	10am – 1pm training course			
Wednesday	8					
Thursday	7					
Friday	6	1	2-3pm health and safety training			
Saturday	5					
Sunday	3					
Total	38	4				

Complete the labour cost account below from the timesheet above:

Labour cost account

	£			£
Bank		Production		
		Production Overheads		
	435			435

 Activity 14

Brown and Jones are a firm of joiners.

They have a workshop and employ six craftsmen. One of the employees is engaged on the production of standard doors for a local firm of builders.

This employee is paid a bonus based on time saved. The time saved is paid at a rate of 50% of the basic hourly rate.

In addition to the bonus, hours worked over the basic 40 per week are paid at time and a half.

In the week ended 13 February 20X1 the following details were available.

Basic hourly rate	£6.00
Time allowed per standard door	2 hours
Doors produced	25
Time worked	45 hours

The employee's gross pay for the week ended 13 February 20X1 is:

A   £270

B   £285

C   £300

D   £315

 Activity 15

The following information relates to direct labour costs incurred during July 20Y0:

Normal time hours worked	8,000 hours
Overtime at time and a half worked	1,500 hours
Overtime at double time worked	1,000 hours
Total hours worked	10,500 hours
Normal time hourly rate	£7 per hour

Overtime premiums paid are included as part of direct labour costs.

The total cost of direct labour for the month of July 20Y0.

A   £91,000

B   £85,750

C   £70,000

D   £73,500

4 Expenses

Activity 16

RFB plc makes wheels for a variety of uses: wheelbarrows, carts, toys, etc.

Complete the following form by putting a tick for each of the cost items into the appropriate column.

	Capital Expenditure	Revenue Expenditure
Repairs to machinery		
Purchase of new delivery vehicle		
Depreciation of delivery vehicle		
Vehicle tax for new vehicle		
Installation of air conditioning unit		
Redecoration of office		

KAPLAN PUBLISHING

5 Absorption and marginal costing

Activity 17

Crescent Feeds Ltd have produced the following set of cost and management accounting figures for its current accounting period.

	£	
Production and sales tonnage	–	2,500 tonnes
Direct labour	102,000	
Admin overheads	16,500	
Direct materials	210,000	
Direct expenses	5,250	
Fixed production overheads	20,400	
Variable production overheads	20,000	
Selling and distribution costs	52,300	
Financial overhead	2,100	

Calculate for the period:

- Prime cost
- Marginal cost
- Absorption cost
- Non-production cost
- Total cost
- Prime cost per tonne of product
- Marginal cost per tonne of product
- Absorption cost per tonne of product
- Total cost per tonne of product

Activity 18

Voliti Limited

Voliti Limited has produced the following budgeted figures for a new product it hopes to launch.

Direct material	£10 per unit
Direct labour	£5 per unit
Variable production overheads	£8 per unit

Fixed production costs	£19,500 per month
Budgeted output	6,500 units per month
Sales price	£30 per unit

Month 1

Production	6,500
Sales	5,000

Task

Complete the profit statement for month 1 on each of the following bases, and reconcile the resulting profit figures:

(i)   marginal costing principles

	£	£
Sales		
Opening Stock		
Marginal costs		
Closing stock	( )	
Cost of sales		( )
Contribution		
Fixed costs		( )
Profit		

(ii)   absorption costing principles

	£	£
Sales		
Opening stock		
Production costs		
Closing stock	( )	
Cost of sales		( )
Gross profit		
Non-production costs		
Profit		

The absorption costing profit is *higher/lower** than the marginal costing profit because there is *more/less** fixed costs charged against the sales in the absorption costing statement.

*delete as appropriate

6 Accounting for overheads

Activity 19

Ray Ltd has the following four production departments:

- Machining 1

- Machining 2

- Assembly

- Packaging

The budgeted fixed overheads relating to the four production departments for Quarter 3 2005 are:

	£	£
Depreciation		80,000
Rent and rates		120,000
Indirect labour costs:		
Machining 1	40,500	
Machining 2	18,300	
Assembly	12,400	
Packaging	26,700	
Total		97,900
Assembly costs	15,600	
Total fixed overheads		313,500

Fixed overheads are allocated or apportioned to the production departments on the most appropriate basis.

The following information is also available:

Department	Net book value of fixed assets (£000)	Square metres occupied	Number of employees
Machining 1	1,280	625	8
Machining 2	320	250	4
Assembly	960	500	3
Packaging	640	1,125	7
Total	3,200	2,500	22

Complete the overhead analysis sheet below (round to the nearest £)

Overhead analysis sheet

	Basis	TOTAL	Machining 1	Machining 2	Assembly	Packaging
Depreciation						
Rent and rates						
Indirect Labour cost						
Assembly costs						
TOTAL						

Activity 20

You have been asked to calculate the under- or over- absorption in a production division, this division is highly automated and operates with expensive machinery, which is run wherever possible on a 24-hour a day, seven days a week basis.

The following information relates to this division for July 20Y0:

Total budgeted departmental overheads	£400,000
Total actual departmental overheads	£450,000
Total budgeted direct labour hours	3,000
Total budgeted machine hours	10,000
Total actual direct labour hours	2,500
Total actual machine hours	9,000

What is the budgeted fixed overhead absorption rate for the division for July 20Y0, using the most appropriate basis of absorption?

A   £50.00

B   £40.00

C   £45.00

D   £44.44

What is the value of the overhead absorbed into production?

A   £500,000

B   £405,000

C   £360,000

D   £444,400

What is the under- or over absorption for the division?

A   £50,000 under

B   £50,000 over

C   £90,000 over

D   £90,000 under

What is the double entry for the above?

A   Dr Production overheads £90,000, Cr Profit and loss £90,000

B   Dr Profit and loss £90,000, Cr Production overheads £90,000

C   Dr Production overheads £50,000, Cr Profit and loss £50,000

D   Dr Profit and loss £50,000, Cr Production overheads £50,000

 Activity 21

R Noble and Sons are a firm of agricultural engineers based in North Yorkshire.

They have a large workshop from which they operate. The business is divided into cost centres which include:

- Machining
- Fabrication
- Canteen
- Stores
- Maintenance

A summary of their budgeted overhead for the three months ended 31 March 20X1 showed:

	£
Depreciation of machinery	5,000
Insurance of machinery	2,100
Heat and light	800
Power	1,750
Rent and rates	2,250
	11,900

Other relevant costs and data for the period showed:

	Machining	Fabrication	Stores	Canteen
No of employees	2	2	1	0
Value of plant	£40,000	£19,000	£2,500	£1,000
Floor area (sq m)	300	350	100	50
Kilowatt hours	600	500	400	250
Material requisitions	195	199	–	–
Direct labour hours	1,600	1,067	–	–

(a) Complete the overhead analysis sheet below (round to the nearest £)

Overhead analysis sheet

	BASIS	TOTAL	PRODUCTION		SERVICE	
			Machining	Fabrication	Stores	Canteen
Dep'n of machinery						
Insurance of machinery						
Heat and light						
Power						
Rent and rates						
Sub-total						
Reapportion canteen						( )
Reapportion stores					( )	
TOTAL						

(b) What would be the overhead rate per kilowatt hour for the production departments is:

	Machining	Fabrication
A	£12.15	£9.22
B	£4.56	£4.32
C	£37.38	£46.57
D	£24.30	£13.17

(c) Based on the OAR calculated above what would be the under or over absorption in each department if the following actually occurred.

The actual Kilowatt hours for the period were: machining 614 hours and fabrication 495 hours.

The actual overhead for the period was: machining £7,960 and fabrication £3,800

	Machining	Fabrication
A	£500 over	£764 under
B	£764 over	£500 under
C	£500 under	£764 over
D	£764 under	£500 over

 Activity 22

During period 5, the month of May 20X1, Lester Bird's under- and over-recovery of overhead per cost centre was:

Cost centre	Overhead absorbed £	Actual overhead £	(under)/over-absorbed £
Painting	3,950	4,250	(300)
Finishing	2,950	3,150	(200)
Trimming	1,640	1,600	40
Firing	2,750	2,600	150
	£11,290	£11,600	(310)

Post the total figures to the overhead account, showing the transfer of the under-absorption to the costing profit and loss account.

Production overhead control account

	£		£
	———		———
	£		£
	———		———

Activity 23

Biscuit Making Company

The general manager has asked you to monitor the absorption of overheads for the production departments for November 20X8.

Company policy is to absorb overheads on the following basis.

Department	Basis
Mixing	Per £ of labour cost
Baking	Machine hours
Packing	Labour hours

Budgeted and actual data for November 20X8 is:

	Mixing	Baking	Packing
Budgeted overheads	£164,000	£228,900	£215,000
Actual labour hours worked			16,000
Budgeted labour hours			17,200
Actual machine hours		16,100	
Budgeted machine hours		16,350	
Actual labour costs	£63,700		
Budgeted labour costs	£65,600		

Calculate the budgeted overhead absorption rate for each department.

	Mixing £	Baking £	Packing £
Budgeted overhead Absorption rate			

Complete the table below.

PRODUCTION OVERHEAD SCHEDULE			
Month:			
	Mixing £	**Baking** £	**Packing** £
Budgeted overheads			
Actual overheads	171,500	224,000	229,000
Overhead absorbed			

Complete the table and production overhead account below.

	Mixing £	**Baking** £	**Packing** £
Over-absorbed overheads			
Under-absorbed overheads			

Production overhead control account

	£		£
	____		____
£	____	£	____

7 Job and batch costing systems

 Activity 24

Billie Millar

The following information relates to the manufacture of product Delphinium during the month of April 2005:

Direct materials per unit	£10.60
Direct labour per unit	£16.40
Total variable overheads	£60,000

Total fixed overheads	£80,000
Number of units produced	10,000

Task

Calculate the prime cost per unit.

Calculate the marginal cost per unit.

Calculate the absorption cost per unit.

 Activity 25

Jetprint Limited

Jetprint Limited specialises in printing advertising leaflets and is in the process of preparing its price list. The most popular requirement is for a folded leaflet made from a single sheet of A4 paper. From past records and budgeted figures, the following data have been estimated for a typical batch of 10,000 leaflets:

Artwork (fixed cost)	£65
Machine setting (fixed cost)	4 hours @ £22 per hour
Paper	£12.50 per 1,000 sheets
Ink and consumables	£40 per 10,000 leaflets
Printers' wages	4 hours @ £8 per hour per 10,000 leaflets

General fixed overheads are £15,000 per period during which a total of 600 printers' labour hours are expected to be worked (not all, of course, on the leaflet). The overheads are recovered only on printers' hours.

Task

Calculate the cost (to the nearest pound) of the leaflets for batches of 10,000 and 20,000 leaflets.

	10,000 leaflets	20,000 leaflets
Artwork		
Machine Setting		
Paper		
Ink and consumables		
Printers' wages		
General fixed overheads		
Total		

8 Process costing

 Activity 26

Mike Everett Ltd produce animal feeds. 'Calfextra' is one of its products. The product is produced in a single process.

The following information relates to week ended 10 February 20X1.

Inputs:	Direct material	720 tonnes at £60 per tonne.
	Direct labour	40 labour hours at £5.20 per hour.
	Overhead	£4.10 per direct labour hour.

Normal loss is based on an allowance of 5% of input and waste has a saleable value of £1 per tonne.

Output for the period was 675 tonnes.

Prepare the process account for the period

Calfextra

	tonnes	£		tonnes	£
Materials			Normal loss		
Labour			Output		
Overhead					
	_____			_____	
	_____			_____	

What is the double entry for the abnormal losses or gains in the above process account?

A   Credit Abnormal loss account, Debit Process account

B   Debit Abnormal loss account, Credit Process account

C   Credit Abnormal gain account, Debit Process account

D   Debit Abnormal gain account, Credit Process account

Activity 27

Mike Everett Ltd produces animal feeds. A further product is 'Pigextra' and this is produced in a single process.

For the week ended 10 March 20X1 the following information was available and related to 'Pigextra' production.

Inputs: Direct material   1,000 tonnes at £17.20 per tonne.

　　　　　Direct labour   280 hours at £10.50 per hour.

　　　　　Overhead   £32 per direct labour hour.

Normal loss allowance is 5% of input and waste is saleable at £12 per tonne.

Output for the period was 1030 tonnes.

Prepare the process account.

Pigextra

	tonnes	£		tonnes	£
Materials			Normal loss		
Labour			Output		
Overhead					
	─────	─────		─────	─────
	─────	─────		─────	─────

What is the double entry for the abnormal losses or gains in the above process account?

A   Credit Abnormal loss account, Debit Process account

B   Debit Abnormal loss account, Credit Process account

C   Credit Abnormal gain account, Debit Process account

D   Debit Abnormal gain account, Credit Process account

Activity 28

Blake Ltd produces a soft drink in a single process. The following information relates to period 1.

Direct material	800 kg at £90.30 per kg
Direct labour	320 hours at £15.50 per hour
Overhead recovery rate	£6 per hour

Normal loss allowance is 3% of input, which can be sold for £63.33 per kg

Finished output	950 kg

There was no opening or closing work in progress

Prepare a process account for the above process.

Process soft drink

	kg	£		kg	£
Materials			Normal loss		
Labour			Output		
Overhead					
	___			___	
	___			___	

 Activity 29

Maston Ltd produces special oil in a single process. The oil is made by introducing 10,000 litres of liquid into a process at a cost of £5 per litre.

The normal loss is 500 litres which can be sold for £1 per litre.

Each process requires £4,000 of labour. The overhead is recovered at 150% of labour.

If there are no abnormal losses or gains, produce the process account for the above.

Process 1

	litres	£		litres	£
Materials			Normal loss		
Labour			Output		
Overhead					
	———			———	
	———			———	

Activity 30

Maston Ltd produces special oil in a single process. The oil is made by introducing 10,000 litres of liquid into a process at a cost of £5 per litre.

The normal loss is 500 litres which can be sold for £1 per litre.

Each process requires £4,000 of labour. The overhead is recovered at 150% of labour.

The output of process 7 is 9,300 litres.

Produce the process account, the abnormal loss/gain account and the normal loss account for process 7.

Process 7

	litres	£		litres	£
Materials			Normal loss		
Labour			Output		
Overhead					
	———			———	
	———			———	

Normal loss account

	£		£
	———		———
	———		———

Abnormal loss/gain account

	£		£
	———		———
	———		———

Activity 31

Egton Farm Supplies Ltd produce fertilisers and chemicals. One of its products 'Eg3' is produced in a single process.

The following information relates to period 5, 20X1.

Inputs:	Direct material	1,000 tonnes of 'X' at £70/tonne.
	Direct labour	60 hours at £8/hour.
	Overhead recovery rate	£4/hour.

Completed output:	800 tonnes
Closing work-in-progress:	200 tonnes

There were no losses in the process.

Work-in-progress degree of completion

Material   100%

Labour   80%

Overhead   80%

Prepare the process account for period 5.

Input	Equivalent units			Costs	Costs per EU (£)
	Completed in period EU	CWIP EU	Total EU	Total costs (£)	
Materials					
Labour					
Overheads					

Process 5					
	tonnes	£		tonnes	£
Materials			WIP		
Labour			Output		
Overhead					
	_____			_____	
	_____			_____	

Activity 32

Taylor

Taylor Ltd makes a product using a number of processes. Details for process 1 during a particular period are as follows:

Inputs	5,000 kilo at £2.47 per kilo
Labour	£1225
Overheads	150% of labour
Completed output:	4750 kilo
Closing work-in-progress:	250 kilo

There were no losses in the process.

Work-in-progress degree of completion

Material	100%
Labour	60%
Overhead	60%

Prepare the process account for period 1

Input	Equivalent units			Costs	Costs per EU (£)
	Completed in period EU	CWIP EU	Total EU	Total costs (£)	
Materials					.
Labour					
Overheads					

Process 5

	kilos	£		kilos	£
Materials			WIP		
Labour			Output		
Overhead					
	_____			_____	
	_____			_____	

Activity 33

Ipako

Ipako produces perfume on a production line. The details of the process in Period 4 are as follows:

OWIP	=	400 units
Costs incurred so far		
Materials	£48,000	
Conversion	£35,500	
Completed output	=	1,200 units
CWIP	=	500 units
Degree of completion:		
Materials	100%	
Conversion	45%	

Costs incurred in Period 1:

Materials	£120,000
Conversion	£78,000

Complete the process accounting using the AVCO method of valuing OWIP

Solution

Equivalent units	Material	Conversion
Completed Output		
CWIP		
Total EU		

Costs		
OWIP		
Period		_____
Total cost		
Cost per EU		
		_____

The costs may now be attributed to the categories of output as follows:

	£	£
Completed units:		
Closing WIP: Materials		
Conversion		
	_____	
		_____
		_____

The process account would appear as follows:

Process account

	£		£
OWIP		Completed goods	
Materials		Closing WIP	
Conversion			
	_____		_____
	_____		_____

 Activity 34

Noil

Noil makes electric cars on a production line. The details of the process in Period 2 are as follows:

OWIP = 250 units

Costs incurred so far

Materials	£54,000
Conversion	£42,000

Degrees of completion

    Materials   100%
    Conversion   60%

Completed output = 3,200 units

CWIP = 230 units

Degree of completion:

    Materials   100%
    Conversion   70%

Costs incurred in Period 1:

    Materials   £135,000
    Conversion   £99,000

Complete the process accounting using the FIFO method of valuing OWIP

Solution

Equivalent units	Material	Conversion
OWIP to complete		
Completed Output		
CWIP		
Total EU		

Costs

Period		
Total cost		

Cost per EU

(to 4 decimal places)

The costs may now be attributed to the categories of output as follows:

	£	£
Completed units: OWIP from previous period		
OWIP completed		
Completed output		
Closing WIP: Materials		
Conversion		

The process account would appear as follows:

Process account

	£		£
OWIP		Completed goods	
Materials		Closing WIP	
Conversion			
	———		———
	———		———

9 Basic variances

Activity 35

Youssef Ltd is preparing it's budget for the next quarter and it needs to consider different production levels.

The semi-variable costs should be calculated using the high-low method. If 3,000 batches are produced then the semi-variable cost will be £17,000.

Complete the table below and calculate the estimated profit per batch at the different activity levels.

Batches sold and produced	1,000	1,500	2,000
Sale Revenue	80,000		
Variable cost			
Direct Materials	8,000		
Direct Labour	7,600		
Overheads	14,400		
Semi-variable costs	9,000		
Variable element			
Fixed element			

KAPLAN PUBLISHING

Fixed cost	7,000		
Total cost	46,000		
Total profit	34,000		
Profit per batch (to 2 decimal places)	34.00		

Activity 36

Yussef Ltd is comparing it's budget for the quarter with the actual revenue and costs incurred (continuation of activity 35).

The semi-variable costs should be calculated using the high-low method. If 3,000 batches are produced then the semi-variable cost will be £8,500.

	Budget	Actual
Volume Sold	1,000	1,200
	£	£
Sale Revenue	80,000	100,000
Less costs:		
Direct Materials	8,000	9,000
Direct Labour	7,600	9,300
Overheads	14,400	17,500
Semi-variable costs	9,000	9,900
Fixed cost	7,000	7,100
Total profit	34,000	47,200

Complete the table below to show a flexed budget and the resulting variances, indicating if it is a favourable (F) or adverse (A) in the final column.

	Flexed Budget	Actual	Variance value	Favourable or Adverse
Volume Sold		1,200		
	£	£	£	
Sale Revenue		100,000		

Less costs:				
Direct Materials		9,000		
Direct Labour		9,300		
Overheads		17,500		
Semi-variable costs		9,900		
Fixed cost		7,100		
Total profit		47,200		

10 Short term decision making

 Activity 37

Which of the following is not a relevant cost/revenue?

A   Variable costs

B   Research and development costs that have already been incurred

C   Incremental fixed costs

D   Increase in sales revenue

 Activity 38

Product	Batman	Robin
Budgeted sales and production	500,000	750,000
Machine hours required	1,000,000	3,750,000
Sales revenue (£)	5,000,000	9,000,000
Direct materials (£)	1,000,000	2,250,000
Direct labour (£)	1,250,000	2,625,000
Variable overheads (£)	1,500,000	1,500,000
Fixed Costs £	1,000,000	2,450,000

The latest sales forecast is that 480,000 units of Product Batman and 910,000 units of Product Robin will be sold during the year.

Complete the table below to calculate the following:

(i)   budgeted breakeven sales, in units, for each of the two products

(ii) the margin of safety (in units) for each of the two products

(iii) the margin of safety as a percentage (to two decimal places).

(iv) If only Robin were made how many would be needed to make a profit of £280,000? (assume fixed costs are product specific)

Product	Batman	Robin
Fixed costs (£)		
Unit contribution (£)		
Breakeven sales (units)		
Forecast sales (units)		
Margin of safety (units)		
Margin of safety (%)		
Target profit (units)		

Activity 39

DH is considering the purchase of a bar/restaurant which is available for £130,000. He has estimated that the weekly fixed costs will be as follows:

	£
Business rates	125
Electricity	75
Insurances	60
Gas	45
Depreciation	125
Telephone	50
Advertising	40
Postage and stationery	20
Motor expenses	20
Cleaning	10

The contribution to sales ratio is 60%.

The weekly breakeven sales value of the business is:

A   £800

B   £970

C   £850

D   £950

 Activity 40

Triproduct Limited makes and sells three types of electronic security systems for which the following information is available.

Expected cost and selling prices per unit

Product	Day scan	Night scan	Omni scan
	£	£	£
Materials	70	110	155
Manufacturing labour	40	55	70
Installation labour	24	32	44
Variable overheads	16	20	28
Selling price	250	320	460

Fixed costs for the period are £450,000 and the installation labour, which is highly skilled, is available for 25,000 hours only in a period and is paid £8 per hour.

Both manufacturing and installation labour are variable costs.

The maximum demand for the products is:

Day scan	Night scan	Omni scan
2,000 units	3,000 units	1,800 units

Determine the best production plan, assuming that Triproduct Limited wishes to maximise profit.

	Day	Night	Omni
Selling price (£)			
Variable cost per unit (£)			
Contribution per unit (£)			
LF per unit (hrs)			
Contribution per LF (£)			
Rank			

Production Plan

Product in rank order	Units	LF per unit (hr)	Total LF (hr)	Contribution (£)
1				
2				
3				
		Total LF	25,000hr	
			Total Contribution	
			Fixed costs	
			Profit	

Activity 41

Burma Limited manufactures two products: Alfie and Boris. Details about the products are as follows.

Sales price and costs per unit	Alfie	Boris
Sales price	£16.20	£22.80
Direct materials	£4.00	£6.00
Direct labour	£2.00	£4.00
Fixed production overheads per unit based on labour hour	£3.00	£6.00
Variable selling costs	£0.50	£0.50
Maximum sales units	10,000 units	15,000 units

Direct materials cost £2 per kilo, and direct labour costs £10 per hour.

In the coming year it is expected that the supply of labour will be limited to 4,000 hours.

Fixed production overhead rates have been calculated using the maximum expected number of labour hours available in the coming period.

State how many units of each product Burma Limited should produce in order to maximise profit.

	Alfie	Boris
Selling price (£)		
Variable cost per unit (£)		
Contribution per unit (£)		
LF per unit (hrs)		
Contribution per LF (£)		
Rank		

Production Plan

Product in rank order	Units	LF per unit (hr)	Total LF (hr)	Contribution (£)
1				
2				
		Total LF	4,000hr	
			Total Contribution	
			Fixed costs	
			Profit	

Activity 42

Naturo Limited can synthesise a natural plant extract called Ipethin into one of three products. Ipethin is in short supply and the company at present is able to obtain only 1,000 kgs per period at a cost of £25 per kg.

The budgeted costs and other data for a typical period are as follows:

	Product A	Product B	Product C
Kgs of Ipethin per unit	1.4	0.96	2.6
Labour hours per unit			
(£8 per hour)	3	8	4
Selling price per unit	£110	£150	£180
Maximum demand (units)	200	400	300

Fixed costs are £25,000 per period.

Task

Determine the preferred order of manufacture in order to maximise profit.

	A	B	C
Selling price (£)			
Variable cost per unit (£)			
Contribution per unit (£)			
LF per unit (kgs)			
Contribution per LF (£)			
Rank			

Production Plan

Product in rank order	Units	LF per unit (kg)	Total LF (kg)	Contribution (£)
1				
2				
3				
		Total LF	1,000kgs	
			Total Contribution	
			Fixed costs	
			Profit	

11 Long term decision making

Activity 43

Highscore Ltd manufacture cricket bats. They are considering investing £30,000 in a new delivery vehicle which will generate savings compared with sub-contracting out the delivery service. The vehicle will have a life of six years, with zero scrap value.

The accounting technician and the transport manager have prepared the following estimates relating to the savings.

The cash flows from the project are:

Year	£
1	9,000
2	11,000
3	10,000
4	10,500
5	10,200
6	10,100

The business cost of capital is 15%.

Required

Prepare an appraisal of the project

	Year 0	Year 1	Year 2	Year 3	Year 4	Year 5	Year 6
Capital expenditure							
Net cash flow							
PV Factor	1.000	0.870	0.756	0.658	0.572	0.497	0.432
Discounted cash flow							
Net present value							

The net present value is *positive/negative**

delete as appropriate

The payback period is   Year(s) and   Months

*Accept/reject** investment

delete as appropriate

Activity 44

Whitby Engineering Factors are considering an investment in a new machine tool with an estimated useful life of five years.

The investment will require capital expenditure of £50,000 and the accounting technician has prepared the following estimates of cash flow over the five-year period:

Year	£
1	18,000
2	20,000
3	21,000
4	22,000
5	18,000

The firm's cost of capital is considered to be 12% and it uses this rate to appraise any future projects.

Required

Prepare an appraisal of the project using the discounted cash flow (NPV method) technique and payback method

	Year 0	Year 1	Year 2	Year 3	Year 4	Year 5
Capital expenditure						
Net cash flow						
PV Factor	1.000	0.893	0.797	0.712	0.636	0.567
Discounted cash flow						
Net present value						

The net present value is *positive/negative**

*delete as appropriate

The payback period is   Year(s) and   Months

*Accept/reject** investment

*delete as appropriate

Activity 45

An investment project has the following expected cash flows over its three-year life span.

Year	Cash flow
	£
0	(285,400)
1	102,000
2	124,000
3	146,000

Task

Calculate the net present value of the project at a discount rate of 20%.

	Year 0	Year 1	Year 2	Year 3
Capital expenditure				
Net cash flow				
PV Factor	1.000	0.833	0.694	0.579
Discounted cash flow				
Net present value				

The net present value is *positive/negative**

*delete as appropriate

The payback period is   Year(s) and   Months

Accept/reject* investment

*delete as appropriate

 Activity 46

Martinez Limited makes a single product, the Angel.

Martinez Limited has a long-term contract to supply a group of customers with 10,000 units of Angel a year for the next three years.

Martinez is considering investing in a new machine to manufacture the Angel. This machine will produce 10,000 units a year, which have a profit of £8 per unit. The machine will cost £220,000 and will last for the duration of the contract. At the end of the contract the machine will be scrapped with no resale value.

KAPLAN PUBLISHING

Task

Calculate the present value of the machine project if a 10% discount rate is used.

	Year 0	Year 1	Year 2	Year 3
Capital expenditure				
Net cash flow				
PV Factor	1.000	0.909	0.826	0.751
Discounted cash flow				
Net present value				

The net present value is *positive/negative**

*delete as appropriate

The payback period is   Year(s) and   Months

Accept/reject* investment

*delete as appropriate

 Activity 47

Loamshire County Council operates a library service.

In order to reduce operating expenses over the next four or five years, there is a proposal to introduce a major upgrade to the computer system used by the library service. Two alternative projects are under examination with different initial outlays and different estimated savings over time. The computer manager has prepared the following schedule:

	Project A £	Project B £
Initial outlay	75,000	100,000
Annual cash savings		
1st year	20,000	30,000
2nd year	30,000	45,000
3rd year	30,000	45,000
4th year	25,000	40,000
5th year	20,000	–

Assume that the cash savings occur at the end of the year, even though in practice they would be spread over the year. From a technical point of view, both systems meet the librarian's specification. It is assumed that there will be no further savings after year 5. The county uses the net present value method for evaluating projects at a 10% discount rate.

Task

Project A

	Year 0	Year 1	Year 2	Year 3	Year 4	Year 5
Capital expenditure						
Net cash flow						
PV Factor	1.000	0.909	0.826	0.751	0.683	0.621
Discounted cash flow						
Net present value						

The net present value is *positive/negative**

*delete as appropriate

The payback period is　　　　　　　Year(s) and　　　　　　　Months

Project B

	Year 0	Year 1	Year 2	Year 3	Year 4
Capital expenditure					
Net cash flow					
PV Factor	1.000	0.909	0.826	0.751	0.683
Discounted cash flow					
Net present value					

The net present value is *positive/negative**

*delete as appropriate

The payback period is　　　　　　　Year(s) and　　　　　　　Months

Invest in *A/B**

*delete as appropriate

KAPLAN PUBLISHING

Activity 48

A transport company is considering purchasing an automatic vehicle-cleansing machine. At present, all vehicles are cleaned by hand.

The machine will cost £80,000 to purchase and install in year 0 and it will have a useful life of four years with no residual value.

The company uses a discount rate of 10% to appraise all capital projects.

The cash savings from the machine will be:

Year	£
0	–
1	29,600
2	29,200
3	28,780
4	28,339

Task

As assistant management accountant, you are asked to carry out an appraisal of the proposal to purchase the machine and prepare a report to the general manager of the company. Your report should contain the following information:

(1)   the net present value of the cash flows from the project

(2)   the payback period of the proposal

(3)   a recommendation as to whether or not the proposal should be accepted.

In your calculations, you should assume that all cash flows occur at the end of the year.

	Year 0	Year 1	Year 2	Year 3	Year 4
Capital expenditure					
Net cash flow					
PV Factor	1.000	0.909	0.826	0.751	0.683
Discounted cash flow					
Net present value					

The net present value is *positive/negative**

*delete as appropriate

The payback period is   Year(s) and   Months

*Accept/reject** project

*delete as appropriate

Activity 49

A company is considering setting up a small in-house printing facility.

Machines costing £14,400 will be purchased in year 0. They will last for four years and will have no value at the end of this time.

The cash savings associated with the machines will be:

Year	£
0	–
1	6,920
2	6,920
3	6,920
4	6,920

Task

(a) Calculate the net present value of the cash flows from the proposal, using a 12% discount rate over four years.

   Assume that all cash flows occur at the end of the year.

(b) Calculate the payback period for the proposal assuming that cash flows occur evenly through the year.

	Year 0	Year 1	Year 2	Year 3	Year 4
Capital expenditure					
Net cash flow					
PV Factor	1.000	0.893	0.797	0.712	0.636
Discounted cash flow					
Net present value					

The net present value is *positive/negative**

*delete as appropriate

The payback period is   Year(s) and   Months

*Accept/reject** project

*delete as appropriate

Activity 50

Data

RBG plc is a large quoted company using a 25% rate of interest for appraising capital projects. One of its divisional directors has put forward plans to make a new product, the AI. This will involve buying a machine specifically for that task. The machine will cost £600,000 and have a life of 5 years. However, because of the nature of the product, the machine will have no residual value at any time.

The annual cash flows will be as follows:

	£
Sales	380,000
Material costs	90,000
Labour costs	30,000
Overhead costs	20,000

Task

You are asked to appraise the divisional director's proposal by calculating :

(a)   the net present value

(b)   the payback period

	Year 0	Year 1	Year 2	Year 3	Year 4	Year 5
Capital expenditure						
Net cash flow						
PV Factor	1.000	0.800	0.640	0.512	0.410	0.328
Discounted cash flow						
Net present value						

The net present value is *positive/negative**

*delete as appropriate

The payback period is   Year(s) and   Months

Further information

The IRR is 20%

The new product *should be/should not be** purchased

*delete as appropriate

Activity 51

Emer Ltd

Emer Ltd is deciding whether to invest in a new machine that will enable them to produce more units to sell. The machine is predicted to increase sales but will also incur some operating costs.

	Year 0	Year 1	Year 2	Year 3
Capital expenditure	30,000			
Sales		15,000	17,000	19,000
Operating costs		5,000	5,500	5,750

Task

Calculate the present value of the machine project if a 12% discount rate is used and the payback period. Complete the report by inserting your own figures or by deleting words as appropriate.

	Year 0	Year 1	Year 2	Year 3
Capital expenditure				
Net cash flow				
PV Factor	1.000	0.909	0.826	0.751
Discounted cash flow				
Net present value				

The net present value is *positive/negative**

*delete as appropriate

The payback period is _____ Year(s) and _____ Months

MEMORANDUM

To:	The divisional accountant
From:	Assistant management accountant
Date:	7 December 20Y0
Subject:	Capital appraisal of new machine

As a result of using discounted cash flow, the net present value of the project is £_____ *positive/negative.* The proposal has a payback of _____ years and _____ months.

The IRR for this project is 15% therefore based on this we should *accept/reject* the project. The IRR of a project is when the NPV equals _____.

Based on the above information the proposal should be *accepted/rejected*.

The value of the net present value represents the *gain/loss* to the company in the equivalent of pounds today from carrying out the proposal.

KAPLAN PUBLISHING

ANSWERS

Key technique answers

1 Principles of cost accounting

 Activity 1

A cost centre is defined as:

B   A production or service location, function, activity or item of equipment for which costs are accumulated.

 Activity 2

Direct costs are:

C   Costs that relate directly to a unit

 Activity 3

A semi-variable cost is:

D   A cost that contains both a fixed and a variable element

 Activity 4

The cost for the electricity for 75 units is:

C   £250

Variable cost

$$\frac{300 - 120}{100 - 10} = £2$$

Fixed cost

300 − (100 × 2) = 100

Cost for 75 units

100 + (75 × 2) = 250

Activity 5

COST	ACTIVITY (Packets)		
	175,000	**200,000**	**225,000**
	£	£	£
Total variable cost	26,250	30,000	33,750
Total fixed cost	58,000	58,000	58,000
Total cost	84,250	88,000	91,750
Cost per packet	0.48	0.44	0.41

The cost per packet has **decreased** because the fixed cost per unit has **decreased**.

2 Material costs

Activity 6

Goods received note	Document completed by stores on receipt of goods
Purchase order	Form completed by the purchasing department to order supplies
Purchase requisition	Form completed by the stores department detailing stock requirements
Stores record card	Document completed to show the movement of stock

KAPLAN PUBLISHING

Delivery note	Form received with goods on delivery
Purchase invoice	Details the amount due to be paid and the date payment is due by

Activity 7

Issues:

		£
15 Jan	30 pairs @ £2	60
29 Jan	35 pairs @ £2	70
Value of issues		130

Closing stock valuation:

		£
(150 – 65)	85 pairs @ £2	170
	40 pairs @ £1.90	76
	125 pairs	246

Double entry for the receipt on the 7th January

C   Dr Materials, Cr Bank

Activity 8

Issues:

		£
Week ending	7 Dec 400 units	
	200 @ £0.90	180
	200 @ £1.00	200
Week ending	14 Dec 350 units	
	350 @ £1.00	350
Week ending	21 Dec 410 units	
	250 @ £1.00	250
	160 @ £0.95	152

Week ending	28 Dec 475 units	
	475 @ £0.95	451
		————
		1,583
		————
Closing stock		
	565 units @ £0.95	£537
		————

Activity 9

	Receipts			Issues			Stock		
	Units	Cost	£	Units	Cost	£	Units	Cost	£
1 Sept							75	40.00	3,000
1 Sept	100	40.00	4,000				175	40.00	7,000
10 Sept	75	42.00	3,150				250	*40.60	10,150
15 Sept				60	40.60	2,436	190		7,714
20 Sept				55	40.60	2,233	135		5,481
23 Sept	45	42.00	1,890				180	*40.95	7,371
30 Sept				50	40.95	2,048	130	40.95	5,323

Value of issues:£6,717

Stock valuation:£5,323

*Weighted average price = $\dfrac{10,150}{250}$ = £40.60

*£7,371/180 = £40.95

Activity 10

Stores Record Card

Material: Sugar   **Month:** May 20X8

Date	Receipts			Issues			Balance		
	Quantity	Price £	Total £	Quantity	Price) £	Total £	Quantity	Price £	Total £
1/5 Balance							2,420	5,200	12,584
7/5	2,950	5.500	16,226				5,370	5.365	28,810
11/5	3,200	5.700	18,239				8,570	5.490	47,049

Date	Receipts Qty	Cost	Total	Issues Qty	Cost	Total	Balance Qty	Cost	Total
14/5				4,105	5.490	22,536	4,465	5.490	24,513
21/5	1,535	5.400	8,289				6,000	5.467	32,802
27/5				1,800	5.467	9,841	4,200	5.467	22,961
30/5				2,600	5.467	14,214	1,600	5.467	8,747

The double entry for the issue on the 27th May is

D   Dr Production, Cr Materials

 ## Activity 11

Navneet Ltd

Identify the method of stock valuation and complete the stock record card shown below for steel component Magic, for the month of May 20Y0.

Valuation method is FIFO

STOCK RECORD CARD FOR STEEL COMPONENT MAGIC								
	Receipts			Issues			Balance	
Date 20Y0	Quantity kg	Cost per kg (£)	Total cost (£)	Quantity kg	Cost per kg (£)	Total cost (£)	Quantity kg	£
Balance as at 1 May							25,000	50,000
9 May	30,000	2.30	69,000				55,000	119,000
12 May				40,000	25,000 @ 2 15,000 @ 2.30	84,500	15,000	34,500
18 May	20,000	2.50	50,000				35,000	84,500
27 May				10,000	2.30	23,000	25,000	61,500

Date 20Y0	Code	Dr £	Cr £
9 May	306	69,000	
9 May	500		69,000
12 May	401	84,500	
12 May	306		84,500
18 May	306	50,000	
18 May	500		50,000
27 May	402	23,000	
27 May	306		23,000

 Activity 12

Ravenscar Engineering

Reorder level:
Maximum usage per period × maximum delivery period
$\quad$ 600 × 6 = 3,600 units

Economic order quantity:
√[(2 × 25 × 500 × 50)/5] = 5000

Maximum stock level:
Reorder level + Reorder quantity – (minimum usage in minimum delivery period)
$\qquad$ = 3,600 + 500 – (400 × 4)
$\qquad$ = 2,500 units

Minimum stock level:
Reorder level – (average usage in average reorder period)
$\qquad$ = 3,600 – (500 × 5)
$\qquad$ = 1,100 units

KAPLAN PUBLISHING

3 Labour costs

📝 ## Activity 13

Employee's weekly timesheet for week ending 24 April

Name:		Ekta Plasm		Cost centre:	Sewing	
Employee number: EP0516				Basic Pay per hour: £9		

	Hours spent on:		Notes	Basic pay £	Overtime premium £	Total pay £
	Production	Indirect work				
Monday	6			54	0	54
Tuesday	3	3	10am – 1pm training course	54	0	54
Wednesday	8			72	6	78
Thursday	7			63	3	66
Friday	6	1	2-3pm health and safety training	63	3	66
Saturday	5			45	18	63
Sunday	3			0	54	54
Total	38	4		351	84	435

Labour cost account

	£		£
Bank	435	Production	315
		Production Overheads	120
	———		———
	435		435
	———		———

Production is **direct** labour cost **only** therefore the cost is:

Basic hours less the time spent spent on non-production activities

£351 – (4 × 9) = £315

Production overheads are the **indirect costs** (the overtime is worked due to general work pressure so is classed as indirect) therefore the cost is:

84 + (4 × 9) = £120

Activity 14

Answer: C

Gross wage:

Basic pay 45 hrs @ £6	£270.00
Overtime 5 hrs @ £3	£15.00

Bonus:

25 doors × 2 hours = 50 hours allowed
Time taken 45 hours
Time saved – 5 hours × £3

	£15.00
	£300.00

Activity 15

Answer: B

Basic pay 10,500 hrs @ £7	£73,500
Overtime 1,500 hrs @3.5	£5,250
Overtime 1,000 hrs @ £7	£7,000
	£85,750

4 Expenses

Activity 16

RFB plc makes wheels for a variety of uses: wheelbarrows, carts, toys, etc.

Complete the following form by putting a tick for each of the cost items into the appropriate column.

	Capital Expenditure	Revenue Expenditure
Repairs to machinery		☑
Purchase of new delivery vehicle	☑	
Depreciation of delivery vehicle		☑
Vehicle tax for new vehicle		☑
Installation of air conditioning unit	☑	
Redecoration of office		☑

5 Absorption and marginal costing

Activity 17

- Prime cost (210,000 + 102,000 + 5,250) — £317,250
- Margin cost (317,250 + 20,000) — £337,250
- Absorption cost (337,250 + 20,400) — £357,650
- Non-production cost (16,500 + 52,300) — £68,800

- Total cost (357,650 + 68,800)   £426,450
- Prime cost per tonne (317,250 ÷ 2,500)   £126.90
- Marginal cost per tonne (337,250 ÷ 2,500)   £134.90
- Absorption cost per tonne (357,650 ÷ 2,500)   £143.06
- Total cost per tonne (426,250 ÷ 2,500)   £170.50

Activity 18

Voliti Limited

(i)   *Marginal costing*

	Units	£	Month 1 £
Sales £30 per unit	5,000		150,000
Opening stock	–	Nil	
Cost of production			
£10 + £5 + £8 = £23	6,500	149,500	
Closing stock £23 each	(1,500)	(34,500)	
Marginal cost of sales	5,000		(115,000)
Contribution			35,000
Fixed costs			(19,500)
Profit			15,500

(ii)   *Absorption costing*

	Units	£	Month 1 £
Sales £30 per unit	5,000		150,000
Opening stock	–	Nil	
Cost of production			
£10 + £5 + £8 + £3 = £26	6,500	169,000	
Closing stock £26 each	(1,500)	(39,000)	
Absorption cost of sales	5,000		(130,000)
Profit			20,000

Working

Fixed overheads absorbed at $\dfrac{£19,500}{6,500 \text{ units}}$ = £3 per unit

Reconciliation of profits

The absorption costing profit is higher than the marginal costing profit because there is less fixed costs charged against the sales in the absorption costing statement.

	£
Profit under marginal costing	15,500
Add: fixed costs carried forward in stock (1,500 × £3)	4,500
Profit under absorption costing	20,000

6   Accounting for overheads

 Activity 19

Ray Ltd has the following four production departments:

- Machining 1
- Machining 2
- Assembly
- Packaging

The budgeted fixed overheads relating to the four production departments for Quarter 3 2005 are:

	£	£
Depreciation		80,000
Rent and rates		120,000
Indirect labour costs:		
Machining 1	40,500	
Machining 2	18,300	
Assembly	12,400	
Packaging	26,700	
Total		97,900
Assembly costs	15,600	
Total fixed overheads		313,500

Fixed overheads are allocated or apportioned to the production departments on the most appropriate basis.

The following information is also available:

Department	Net book value of fixed assets (£000)	Square metres occupied	Number of employees
Machining 1	1,280	625	8
Machining 2	320	250	4
Assembly	960	500	3
Packaging	640	1,125	7
Total	3,200	2,500	22

Complete the overhead analysis sheet below (round to the nearest £)

Overhead analysis sheet

	Basis	TOTAL	Machine 1	Machine 2	Assembly	Packaging
Dep'n	NBV	80,000	32,000	8,000	24,000	16,000
Rent and rates	Square meters	120,000	30,000	12,000	24,000	54,000
Indirect Labour cost	Allocated	97,900	40,500	18,300	12,400	26,700
Assembly costs	Allocated	15,600	-	-	15,600	-
TOTAL		313,500	102,500	38,300	76,000	96,700

Activity 20

What is the budgeted fixed overhead absorption rate for the division for July 20Y0, using the most appropriate basis of absorption?

    B   £40.00

£400,000 ÷ 10,000

What is the value of the overhead absorbed into production?

    C   £360,000

£40 × 9,000

What is the under- or over absorption for the division?

    D   £90,000 under

£450,000 - £360,000

What is the double entry for the above?

    B   Dr Profit and loss £90,000, Cr Production overheads £90,000

 Activity 21

(a) Overhead analysis sheet

	BASIS	TOTAL	PRODUCTION		SERVICE	
			Machining	Fabrication	Stores	Canteen
Dep'n of machinery	Value	5,000	3,200	1,520	200	80
Insurance of machinery	Value	2,100	1,344	638	84	34
Heat and light	Square metres	800	300	350	100	50
Power	Kw	1,750	600	500	400	250
Rent and rates	Square metres	2,250	844	984	281	141
Sub-total		11,900	6,288	3,992	1,065	555
Reapportion canteen	Staff		222	222	111	(555)
Reapportion stores	Requisitions		780	396	(1176)	
TOTAL			7,290	4,610		

(b)   What would be the overhead rate per kilowatt hour for the production departments is:

	Machining	Fabrication
A	£12.15	£9.22

(c)

	Machining	Fabrication
C	£500 under	£764 over

Machining actual = £7,960

Machining absorbed = £12.15 × 614 =   £7,460

Under absorption   £500

Fabrication actual =   £3,800

Fabrication absorbed = £9.22 × 495 =   £4,564

Over absorption   £764

Activity 22

Production overhead control account

	£		£
Actual overhead	11,600	Absorbed overhead	11,290
		Under-absorbed	
		Costing P/L	310
	11,600		11,600

Activity 23

	Mixing £	Baking £	Packing £
Budgeted overhead Absorption rate	£2.50 per £1 direct labour	£14 per machine hour	£12.50 per labour hour

PRODUCTION OVERHEAD SCHEDULE

Month: November 1998

	Mixing £	Baking £	Packing £
Budgeted overheads	164,000	228,900	215,000
Actual overheads	171,500	224,000	229,000
Overhead absorbed	159,250	225,400	200,000

	Mixing £	Baking £	Packing £
Over-absorbed overheads		1,400	
Under-absorbed overheads	12,250		29,000

Production overhead control account

	£		£
Actual overhead	624,500	Absorbed overhead	584,650
		Under absorbed	39,850
	624,500		624,500

7 Job and batch costing

Activity 24

Billie Millar

The following information relates to the manufacture of product Delphinium during the month of April 2005:

Direct materials per unit	£10.60
Direct labour per unit	£16.40
Total variable overheads	£60,000
Total fixed overheads	£80,000
Number of units produced	10,000

Task

Calculate the prime cost per unit.

10.60 + 16.40 = £27.00

Calculate the marginal cost per unit.

27.00 + (60,000 ÷ 10,000) = £33.00

Calculate the absorption cost per unit.

33.00 + (80,000 ÷ 10,000) = £41.00

Activity 25

Jetprint Limited

	Cost of batch 10,000 leaflets	Cost of batch 20,000 leaflets
	£	£
Artwork	65.00	65.00
Machine setting	88.00	88.00
Paper	125.00	250.00
Ink and consumables	40.00	80.00
Printers' wages	32.00	64.00
General fixed overheads (W)	100.00	200.00
Total cost	450.00	747.00

Workings

$$OAR = \frac{£15,000}{600} = £25 \text{ per hour}$$

10,000 leaflets £25 × 4 hours = £100

20,000 leaflets £25 × 8 hours = £200

8 Process costing

Activity 26

Mike Everett Ltd – 'Calfextra'

Determination of losses/gains:

	Tonnes
Input	720
Normal loss 5% of input	36
Normal output	684
Actual output	675
Difference = abnormal loss	9

Calfextra

	tonnes	£		tonnes	£
Material	720	2,400	Normal loss	36	36
Labour		208	Output	675	2,700
Overhead		164	Abnormal loss	9	36
	720	2,772		720	2,772

Normal cost of normal production:

$$\frac{£2772 - £36}{720 - 36} = \frac{£2,736}{684}$$

$$= £4 \text{ per tonne}$$

Output	$675 \times £4$	= £2,700
Abnormal loss	$9 \times £4 =$	£36

The double entry for the abnormal losses in the above process account is:

B   Debit Abnormal loss account, Credit Process account

Activity 27

Mike Everett Ltd – 'Pigextra'

Determination of losses/gains:

	Tonnes
Input	1,000
Normal loss 5% of input	50
Normal output	950
Actual output	1030
Difference = abnormal gain	80

Pigextra

	tonnes	£		tonnes	£
Material	1,000	17,200	Normal loss	50	600
Labour		2,940	Output	1,030	30,900
Overhead		8,960			
Abnormal gain	80	2,400			
	1,080	31,500		1,080	31,500

Normal cost of normal production:

$$\frac{£29,100 - £600}{1,000 - 50} = \frac{£28,500}{950}$$

$$= £30 \text{ per tonne}$$

Output	1030 tonnes × £30	= £30,900
Abnormal gain	80 tonnes × £30	= £2,400

The double entry for the abnormal gain in the above process account is:

C   Credit Abnormal gain account, Debit Process account

Activity 28

Process soft drink

	Kg	£	Date	Kg	£
Material	800	72,240	Normal loss	24	1,520
Labour		4,960	Output	792	79,200
Overhead		1,920			
Abnormal gain	16	1,600			
	816	80,720		816	80,720

Normal cost of normal output $\dfrac{79,120 - 1,520}{800 - 24}$ =

= £100 per Kg

Cost of output = 792 × £100 = £79,200

Cost of abnormal gain = 16 × £100 = £1,600

Activity 29

Process 1

	Litre	£		Litre	£
Direct material	10,000	50,000	Normal loss	500	500
Direct labour		4,000	Output	9,500	59,500
Overhead		6,000			
	10,000	60,000		10,000	60,000

Activity 30

Process 7

	Litre	£		Litre	£
Direct material	10,000	50,000	Normal loss	500	500
Direct labour		4,000	Output	9,300	58,247
Overhead		6,000	Abnormal loss (W1)	200	1,253
	10,000	60,000		10,000	60,000

Normal loss account

	£		£
Process	500	Cash	700
Abnormal loss (W2)			
	700		700

Abnormal loss account

	£		£
Process (W1)	1,253	Normal loss (W2)	200
		Profit and loss	1,053
	1,253		1,253

Working 1

Normal cost of normal output = $\dfrac{59,500}{9,500}$ = £6.2631 per litre.

Therefore, output and the abnormal loss are both costed at £6.2631 per litre.

Working 2

When abnormal loss is transferred to by sold as scrap it is valued at it's scrap value – 200 Litres @ £1 per litre.

Activity 31

Egton Farm Supplies Ltd

Process account

	Units	£		Units	£
Material	1,000	70,000	Output	800	56,600
Labour		480	Work-in-progress	200	14,120
Overhead		240			
	1,000	70,720		1,000	70,720

Work-in-progress valuation

Statement of equivalent units and statement of cost

Element of cost	Comp output	WIP	Equivalent units	Cost £	Cost per unit
Direct materials	800	200	1,000	70,000	70.00
Direct labour	800	160	960	320	0.50
Overhead	800	160	960	160	0.25
					£70.75

Valuation of output and work-in-progress

		£
Completed output 800 tonnes × £70.75		56,600

Work-in-progress

Direct materials	200 tonnes × £70.00	14,000
Direct labour	160 tonnes × £0.50	80
Overhead	160 tonnes × £0.1666	40
		14,120

Activity 32

Taylor

Work-in-progress valuation

Statement of equivalent units and statement of cost

Element of cost	Comp output	WIP	Equivalent units	Cost £	Cost per unit
Direct materials	4,750	250	5,000	12,350	£2.47
Direct labour	4,750	150	4,900	1,225	£0.25
Overhead	4,750	150	4,900	1,837.50	£0.375
					£3.095

Valuation of output and work-in-progress

		£
Completed output 4750 tonnes × £3.095		14,701.25

Work-in-progress

Direct materials	250 tonnes × £2.47	617.50
Direct labour	150 tonnes × £0.25	37.5
Overhead	150 tonnes × £0.375	56.25
		711.25

Process 1 account

	kg	£		kg	£
Materials	5,000	12,350	WIP	250	711.25
Labour		1,225	Output	4,750	14,701.25
Overheads		1,837.50			
Total	5,000	15,412.50	Total	5,000	15,412.50

Activity 33

Equivalent units		Material	Conversion
	Completed Output	1,200	1,200
	CWIP	500	225
	Total EU	1,700	1,425
Costs			
	OWIP	48,000	35,500
	Period	120,000	78,000
	Total cost	168,600	113,500
Cost per EU		£98.82	£79.65

The costs may now be attributed to the categories of output as follows:

		£	£
Completed units:	Completed output 1,200 × £178.47		214,164
Closing WIP:	Materials 500 × £98.82	49,410	
	Conversion 225 × £79.65	17,921	
			67,331
			281,495

The process account would appear as follows:

Process account

	£		£
OWIP	83,500	Completed goods	214,164
Materials	120,000	Closing WIP	67,331
Conversion	78,000	Rounding	5
	281,500		281,500

Activity 34

OWIP + Started = > Completed + CWIP
250 + 3,270 = > 3,200 + 230

The completed units consist of 250 OWIP that were completed this period and then a further 2,950 units that were started and finished in this period.

To complete the OWIP no more material is required but 40% more conversion is needed.

Equivalent units		Material	Conversion
	OWIP to complete	0 (250 - 250 ×100%)	100 (250 – 200 × 60%)
	Completed Output	2,950	2,950
	CWIP	230	161
	Total EU	3,180	3,211
Costs			
	Period	135,000	99,000
	Total cost	135,000	99,000
Cost per EU (to 4 decimal places)		£42.4528	£30.8315

The costs may now be attributed to the categories of output as follows:

		£	£
Completed units:	OWIP from previous period	96,000	
	OWIP completed 100 × £30.8315	3,083	
	Completed output 2,950 × £73.2843	216,189	
			315,272
Closing WIP:	Materials 230 × £42.4528	9,764	
	Conversion 161 × £30.8315	4,964	
			14,728
			330,000

KAPLAN PUBLISHING

The process account would appear as follows:

Process account

	£		£
OWIP	96,000	Completed goods	315,272
Materials	135,000	Closing WIP	14,728
Conversion	99,000		
	330,000		330,000

9 Basic variances

Activity 35

Batches sold and produced	1,000	1,500	2,000
Sale Revenue	80,000	120,000	160,000
Variable cost			
Direct Materials	8,000	12,000	16,000
Direct Labour	7,600	11,400	15,200
Overheads	14,400	21,600	28,800
Semi-variable costs	9,000		
Variable element		6,000	8,000
Fixed element		5,000	5,000
Fixed cost	7,000	7,000	7,000
Total cost	46,000	63,000	80,000
Total profit	34,000	57,000	80,000
Profit per batch (to 2 decimal places)	34.00	38.00	40.00

Splitting the semi-variable cost

Variable cost per unit

$\dfrac{17,000 - 9,000}{3,000 - 1,000} = £4$

Total Fixed cost

$17,000 - (3,000 \times 4) = £5,000$

Variable cost for 1,500 units

$1,500 \times 4 = £6,000$

Variable cost for 2,000 units

$2,000 \times 4 = £8,000$

Activity 36

	Flexed Budget	Actual	Variance value	Favourable or Adverse
Volume Sold	1,200	1,200		
	£	£	£	
Sale Revenue	96,000	100,000	4,000	F
Less costs:				
Direct Materials	9,600	9,000	600	F
Direct Labour	9,120	9,300	180	A
Overheads	17,280	17,500	220	A
Semi-variable costs	9,800	9,900	100	A
Fixed cost	7,000	7,100	100	A
Total profit	43,200	47,200	4,000	F

Calculating the semi-variable cost

$5,000 + (1,200 \times 4) = £9,800$

10 Short term decision making

Activity 37

Which of the following is not a relevant cost/revenue?

B   Research and development costs that have **already been incurred**

This is a sunk cost and not relevant to a future decision

Activity 38

Product	Batman	Robin
Fixed costs (£)	1,000,000	2,450,000
Unit contribution (£)	2.50	3.50
Breakeven sales (units)	400,000	700,000
Forecast sales (units)	480,000	910,000
Margin of safety (units)	80,000	210,000
Margin of safety (%)	16.67%	23.08%
Target profit (units)		780,000

Unit contribution

Calculate the revenue and each variable cost per unit based on budget. Sales revenue less variable costs = contribution

Batman   £5 – (1 + 1.25 + 1.5) = £1.25

Robin   £12 – (3 + 3.5 + 2) = £3.50

Target profit

$\dfrac{2,450,000 + 280,000}{£3.50}$ = 780,000 units of Robin

Activity 39

Answer is D £950

Weekly fixed costs are £570; C/S ratio is 0.6 therefore weekly breakeven sales £570/0.6 = £950

Activity 40

	Day scan £	Night scan £	Omni scan £
Selling price	250	320	460
Variable costs			
Materials	(70)	(110)	(155)
Manufacturing labour	(40)	(55)	(70)
Installation labour	(24)	(32)	(44)
Variable overheads	(16)	(20)	(28)
Contribution per unit	100	103	163
Installation hours required	3	4	5.5
Contribution per installation hour	£33.33	£25.75	£29.64
Production priority	1st	3rd	2nd

Best production plan

	Units	Hours used
Day scan to maximum demand	2,000 (× 3)	6,000
Omni scan to maximum demand	1,800 (× 5.5)	9,900

This leaves (25,000 – 6,000 – 9,900) = 9,100 installation labour hours for Night scan

Therefore production of Night scan = $\dfrac{9,100}{4}$ = 2,275 units

	Day scan	Omni scan	Night scan	Total
Units	2,000	1,800	2,275	
	£	£	£	£
Contribution	200,000	293,400	234,325	727,725
Fixed costs				(450,000)
Maximum profit				277,725

KAPLAN PUBLISHING

Activity 41

	Alfie £		Boris £
Sales price per unit	16.20		22.80
Variable costs per unit	4.00 + 2.00 + 0.50 = 6.50	6.00 + 4.00 + 0.50 =	10.50
Contribution per unit	9.70		12.30
Labour hours per unit	(£2/£10) 0.2	(£4/£10)	0.4
Contribution per labour hour	£48.50		£30.75

Conclusion: manufacture as many units of Alfie as possible.

This requires 10,000 × 0.2 = 2,000 hours

The remaining 4,000 − 2,000 = 2,000 hours can be used to produce units of Boris

This allows 5,000 units of Boris to be made.

We therefore produce 10,000 units of Alfie and 5,000 units of Boris.

	A £	B £	Total £
Contribution	97,000	61,500	158,500
Fixed costs (W1)			(60,000)
Profit			98,500

Working

(W1) *Fixed production overheads*

Using (say) product A: fixed overheads per unit = £3; Labour hours per unit = 0.2.

Thus fixed overheads per hour = £3/0.2 = £15.

Maximum hours available = 4,000.

Fixed production overheads budgeted at 4,000 × £15 = £60,000.

Activity 42

	Product		
	A	B	C
	£	£	£
Selling price	110	150	180
Ipethin (material)	(35)	(24)	(65)
Labour	(24)	(64)	(32)
Contribution	51	62	83
Limiting factor (kg of Ipethin)	1.4	0.96	2.6
Contribution per unit of limiting factor	£36.43	£64.58	£31.92
Preferred order of manufacture	2	1	3

Best production plan

	Units	kg used
B to maximum demand	400 (× 0.96)	384
A to maximum demand	200 (× 1.4)	280

This leaves (1,000 – 384 – 280) = 336kgs for C

Therefore production of C = $\dfrac{336}{2.6}$ = 129 units

	A	B	C	Total
Units	400	200	129	
	£	£	£	£
Contribution	10,200	24,800	10,707	45,707
Fixed costs				(25,000)
Maximum profit				20,707

11 Long term decision making

Activity 43

	Year 0	Year 1	Year 2	Year 3	Year 4	Year 5	Year 6
Capital expenditure	(30,000)						
Net cash flow	(30,000)	9,000	11,000	10,000	10,500	10,200	10,100
PV Factor	1.000	0.870	0.756	0.658	0.572	0.497	0.432
Discounted cash flow	(30,000)	7830	8316	6580	6006	5069	4363
Net present value	8164						

The net present value is *positive*

The payback period is   **3**   Year(s) and   **0**   Months

Year	Cash flow	Cumulative cash flow
0	(30,000)	(30,000)
1	9,000	(21,000)
2	11,000	(10,000)
3	10,000	0

Accept

Activity 44

	Year 0	Year 1	Year 2	Year 3	Year 4	Year 5
Capital expenditure	(50,000)					
Net cash flow	(50,000)	18,000	20,000	21,000	22,000	18,000
PV Factor	1.000	0.893	0.797	0.712	0.636	0.567
Discounted cash flow	(50,000)	16,074	15,940	14,952	13,992	10,206
Net present value	21,164					

The net present value is **positive**

The payback period is   **2**   Year(s) and **6.9**   Months

Year	Cash flow	Cumulative cash flow
0	(50,000)	(50,000)
1	18,000	(32,000)
2	20,000	(12,000)
3	21,000	9,000
4	22,000	

12,000/21,000 × 12 = 6.9 months

Accept

Activity 45

	Year 0	Year 1	Year 2	Year 3
Capital expenditure	(285,400)			
Net cash flow	(285,400)	102,000	124,000	146,000
PV Factor	1.000	0.833	0.694	0.579
Discounted cash flow	(285,400)	84,966	86,056	84,534
Net present value	(29,844)			

The net present value is **negative**

The payback period is   **2**   Year(s) and **4.9**   Months

Year	Cash flow	Cumulative cash flow
0	(285,400)	(285,400)
1	102,000	(183,400)
2	124,000	(59,400)
3	146,000	86,600

59,400/146,000 × 12 = 4.9 months

This project has a negative NPV but still pays back within the life of the project. This project should be **rejected** as when the time value of money is considered there is not a return from the investment

Activity 46

	Year 0	Year 1	Year 2	Year 3
Capital expenditure	(220,000)			
Net cash flow	(220,000)	80,000	80,000	80,000
PV Factor	1.000	0.909	0.826	0.751
Discounted cash flow	(220,000)	72,720	66,080	60,080
Net present value	(21,120)			

The net present value is *negative*

The payback period is **2** Year(s) and **9** Months

Year	Cash flow	Cumulative cash flow
0	(220,000)	(220,000)
1	80,000	(140,000)
2	80,000	(60,000)
3	80,000	20,000

60,000/80,000 × 12 = 9 months

This project has a negative NPV but stil pays back within the life of the project. This project should be **rejected** as when the time value of money is considered there is not a return from the investment.

Activity 47

Project A

	Year 0	Year 1	Year 2	Year 3	Year 4	Year 5
Capital expenditure	(75,000)					
Net cash flow	(75,000)	20,000	30,000	30,000	25,000	20,000
PV Factor	1.000	0.909	0.826	0.751	0.683	0.621
Discounted cash flow	(75,000)	18,180	24,780	22,530	17,075	12,420
Net present value	19,985					

The net present value is *positive*

The payback period is **2** Year(s) and **10** Months

Year	Cash flow	Cumulative cash flow
0	(75,000)	(75,000)
1	20,000	(55,000)
2	30,000	(25,000)
3	30,000	5,000

25,000/30,000 × 12 = 10 months

Project B

	Year 0	Year 1	Year 2	Year 3	Year 4
Capital expenditure	(100,000)				
Net cash flow	(100,000)	30,000	45,000	45,000	40,000
PV Factor	1.000	0.909	0.826	0.751	0.683
Discounted cash flow	(100,000)	27,270	37,170	33,795	27,320
Net present value	25,555				

The net present value is *positive*

The payback period is **2** Year(s) and **6.7** Months

Year	Cash flow	Cumulative cash flow
0	(100,000)	(100,000)
1	30,000	(70,000)
2	45,000	(25,000)
3	45,000	20,000

25,000/45,000 × 12 = 6.7 months

Project **B** should be invested in.

Project B should be recommended as it has the higher discounted cash flow, therefore the higher return from the investment. Payback is a cruder method of assessing future cash flows. No account taken of flows after the payback period and equal weight given to flows within the payback period.

KAPLAN PUBLISHING

Activity 48

	Year 0	Year 1	Year 2	Year 3	Year 4
Capital expenditure	(80,000)				
Net cash flow	(80,000)	29,600	29,200	28,780	28,339
PV Factor	1.000	0.909	0.826	0.751	0.683
Discounted cash flow	(80,000)	26,906	24,119	21,614	19,356
Net present value	11,995				

The net present value is *positive*

The payback period is **2** Year(s) and **8.8** Months

Year	Cash flow	Cumulative cash flow
0	(80,000)	(80,000)
1	29,600	(50,400)
2	29,200	(21,200)
3	28,780	7,580

21,200/28,780 × 12 = 8.8 months

Accept

Activity 49

	Year 0	Year 1	Year 2	Year 3	Year 4
Capital expenditure	(14,400)				
Net cash flow	(14,400)	6,920	6,920	6,920	6,920
PV Factor	1.000	0.893	0.797	0.712	0.636
Discounted cash flow	(14,400)	6,180	5,515	4,927	4,401
Net present value	6,623				

The net present value is *positive*

The payback period is **2** Year(s) and **1** Month

Year	Cash flow	Cumulative cash flow
0	(14,400)	(14,400)
1	6,920	(7480)
2	6,920	(560)
3	6,920	6,360

560/6,920 × 12 = 1 month

Accept

 ## Activity 50

	Year 0	Year 1	Year 2	Year 3	Year 4	Year 5
Capital expenditure	(600,000)					
Net cash flow	(600,000)	240,000	240,000	240,000	240,000	240,000
PV Factor	1.000	0.800	0.640	0.512	0.410	0.328
Discounted cash flow	(600,000)	192,000	153,600	122,880	98,400	78,720
Net present value	45,600					

The net present value is *positive*

*delete as appropriate

The payback period is **2** Year(s) and **6** Months

Year	Cash flow	Cumulative cash flow
0	(600,000)	(600,000)
1	240,000	(360,000)
2	240,000	(120,000)
3	240,000	120,000

120,000/240,000 × 12 = 6 months

The new product *should be* purchased.

Activity 51

Emer Ltd

	Year 0	Year 1	Year 2	Year 3
Capital expenditure	(30,000)			
Net cash flow		10,000	11,500	13,250
PV Factor	1.000	0.893	0.797	0.712
Discounted cash flow	(30,000)	8,930	9,166	9,434
Net present value	(2,470)			

The net present value is *negative*

The payback period is   2   Year(s) and 7.7 Months

Year	Cash flow	Cumulative cash flow
0	(30,000)	(30,000)
1	10,000	(20,000)
2	11,500	(8,500)
3	13,250	4,750

8,500/13,250 × 12 = 7.7 months

M E M O R A N D U M

To: The divisional accountant
From: Assistant management accountant
Date: 7 December 20Y0
Subject: Capital appraisal of new machine

As a result of using discounted cash flow, the net present value of the project is **£2,470 negative.** The proposal has a payback of **2** years and **7.7** months.

The IRR for this project is 15% therefore based the IRR alone we should *accept* the project. The IRR of a project is when the NPV equals **zero**.

Based on the above information the proposal should be *rejected*.

The value of the net present value represents the *loss* to the company in the equivalent of pounds today from carrying out the proposal.

KAPLAN PUBLISHING

Glossary

Term	Description
Abnormal gain	The amount by which normal loss exceeds actual loss.
Abnormal loss	The amount by which actual loss exceeds normal loss.
Absorption costing	Stock units are valued at variable cost plus fixed production overheads absorbed using a pre-determined absorption rate.
Batch costing	The costing system used for a business where production is made up of different product batches of identical units.
Bonus scheme	A day rate combined with a bonus based on output achieved.
Breakeven point	The level of activity required to make no profit and no loss.
Buffer stock	Stock held to cover variations in: – lead time, and – demand during the lead time. Sometimes defined as 'stock held in excess of average units demanded in average lead time'.
Capital expenditure	Expenditure on the purchase or improvement of fixed assets, appearing in the balance sheet.
Contribution	Sales revenue less variable cost of sales.
Cost absorption	The charging of overhead costs to cost units.
Cost accounting	The analysis of costs and revenues to provide useful information to assist the management accounting function.
Cost allocation	The charging of overhead costs to the specific cost centre that incurred them.
Cost apportionment	The splitting of shared overhead costs between relevant cost centres using an appropriate basis.

Term	Description
Cost centre	A location, function, activity or item of equipment in respect of which costs are accumulated.
Cost coding	The allocation of a unique code to costs, usually on the source documentation, to allow accurate and detailed analysis.
Cost unit	An individual unit of product or service for which costs can be separately ascertained.
Cost-volume-profit (CVP) analysis	Analysis of the effects of changes of volume on contribution and profit.
Depreciation	An annual internal charge to the profit and loss account that spreads the net cost of a fixed asset over the number of years of its useful life.
Direct costs	Costs that can be related directly to a cost unit.
Direct expenses	Expenses that can be related specifically to a cost centre.
Discounted cash flow	An investment appraisal technique which discounts future cash flows to a present value.
Economic batch quantity (EBQ)	To minimise the total of the inventory costs.
Economic order quantity (EOQ)	The quantity to be ordered/produced.
Equivalent unit	The number of whole units to which a partially completed unit is equivalent (= physical units × percentage completion).
Expenses	Items of expenditure that are not labour or materials related.
FIFO	A method of valuing issues of stock that assumes that issues are made from the oldest stock available (First In First Out).
Financial accounting	The production of an historic record of transactions presented in a standard format for use by parties external to the business.
Fixed costs	Costs that vary with time, not activity level.
Idle time	Paid for, but non-productive, hours.

KAPLAN PUBLISHING

Term	Description
Integrated bookkeeping system	A bookkeeping system whereby ledger accounts are kept that provide the necessary information for both costing and financial accounting.
Internal rate of return	The rate of interest which will cause the stream of cash flows discounted at that rate of interest to have a nil net present value.
Job costing	The costing system used for a business where production is made up of individual, different, large jobs.
Key factor analysis	The technique of allocating resources between products according to contribution per unit of resource.
Lead time	The time between an order for goods being placed and the receipt of that order.
LIFO	A method of valuing issues of stock that assumes that issues are made from the newest stock available (Last In First Out).
Management accounting	The generation, presentation and interpretation of historic, budgeted and forecast information for management for the purposes of planning, control and decision-making.
Margin of safety	The amount by which the level of activity can fall below budget before a loss is made.
Marginal costing	Stock units are valued at variable production cost; fixed overheads are accounted for as period costs.
Normal loss	The level of expected loss of input from a process.
Over/under absorption (recovery)	Where the amount of overhead absorbed into cost units, using the pre-determined absorption rate, is more/less than the overheads actually incurred.
P/V (C/S) ratio	The ratio of contribution to sales value.
Payback period	The amount of time it takes for an investment project to recover the cash cost of the original investment.
Piecework rates	Where a constant fixed amount is paid per unit of output.

Term	Description
Present value	The value at today's date of an amount of cash received/paid at some time in the future, taking account of the compound interest earned over the relevant period.
Re-order level	The quantity of stock in hand at the time when a new order is placed.
Re-order quantity	The quantity of stock ordered. (Be careful to distinguish between re-order level and re-order quantity.)
Revenue expenditure	Expenditure on goods and services that will be charged to the profit and loss account.
Secondary apportionment	The re-apportionment of service cost centres' overhead costs to production cost centres.
Semi-variable costs	Costs with both a fixed and variable element.
Stock control	The method of ensuring that the right quantity of the right quality of stock is available at the right time and the right place.
Stock control levels	Key stock quantities that assist in stock control, including re-order level, economic order quantity (EOQ), minimum and maximum stock levels.
Stock-outs	Occasions when one or more items of stock are needed but there are none in stock.
Stores record card	A record kept for each stock line, detailing receipts, issues and balance on hand, in terms of both physical quantities and monetary value.
Timesheet	A record of how an employee has spent his/her time, split between jobs/clients and non-productive time.
Usage	The quantity of items required for sale (in the case of goods for resale) or production (in the case of components or raw materials) in a given period.
Variable costs	Costs that vary in direct proportion to the level of activity.
Weighted average cost	A method of valuing issues of stock that takes account of the relative quantities of stock available purchased at different prices.

KAPLAN PUBLISHING

INDEX